The Place I Call Home

Voices and Faces
of
Homeless Teens

The Place I Call Home

Voices and Faces
of
Homeless Teens

Lois Stavsky and I.E. Mozeson

Photographs by Bob Hirschfield

SHAPOLSKY PUBLISHERS, INC.
NEW YORK

A Shapolsky Book

For any additional information, contact:
Shapolsky Publishers, Inc.
136 West 22nd Street, New York, NY 10011

Library of Congress Cataloging in Publication Data

10 9 8 7 6 5 4 3 2 1

ISBN 0-944007-81-3

Book Design and Typography by The Bartlett Press, Inc.,
Somerset, New Jersey

Dedications

Lois Stavsky:
I dedicate this book to my parents, Elliott and Ruth Stavsky, to
my children, Dani and Sara, and to my students.

Bob Hirschfield:
To Maura and Terry.

I.E. Mozeson:
To my family and to the young people who shared so
much in making this book possible.

Fighting homelessness begins at home, and it is our hope that love can
somehow heal the many torn families that are depicted here. If we can
acknowledge and address the many severe problems that emerge from
these teen monologues, the American family can eventually regroup and
stop the cycle of social decay that threatens our nation.

Contents

Preface

After fifteen years of teaching English to "mainstream" students, I began working in the mid-eighties in a dropout prevention program on the Lower East Side of Manhattan. My students and I explored many of the searing urban issues of the day that personally affected most of the classroom. The home neighborhood for many of these youngsters was "Alphabet City," a dingy web of lower-income projects and tenements between Avenues A and D.

During the spring 1989 semester, for a special project that would lead to a published magazine, we focused on homelessness. Several members of the class knew youngsters their own age who were currently living in shelters and welfare hotels. We planned and drafted a set of interview questions. Student investigators set out to capture the facts and feelings behind teenage homelessness.

Homelessness got expanded to other forms of alternate home situations, as young people who had spent time in drug rehab centers, correctional facilities, psychiatric wards and group homes came forward to share their stories. Many of them made a point of saying how they had never told the truth to anyone before, certainly not social workers who they feared would separate them from their families.

My co-author and I helped transcribe the tape recordings that the students obtained and we were inspired to pursue several leads ourselves.

The result is *The Place I Call Home*.

Lois Stavsky

Acknowledgments

Among the people to thank are Shirley Franklin of Federation Employment Guidance Services; Margaret McDermott who taught at the Prince George Hotel; Steve Ashkinazy of the Hetrick Martin Institute; Linda Ortiz, Recreational Director, and the children of the Saratoga Interfaith Family Inn; and Angel Rodriguez, director of the Robert Seigel Center. This book, of course, could not have been done without the student interviewers, especially Lisette Belliard and Violet Matos. Those who gave significant feedback to the manuscript in progress include Ellen Eichel, Miriam Rodgers and Bonnie Rothchild. My children Dani and Sara were avid and encouraging readers.

Our "Homeless" manuscript found a home with a house that is willing to take chances on controversial material. Ian Shapolsky believes in the significance of this book and is not concerned that several institutions stand indicted by the powerful content and implications of its collective testimony. We are grateful, too, for the friendly help of Ann Cassouto and Brian Feinblum at Shapolsky Publishers.

Introduction

"How does it feel,
to be on your own,
with no direction home,
like a rolling stone?"
—Bob Dylan

It can't feel good. Especially when you're only a teenager, barely past the years where life should be a comforting cocoon, and just before the age when you are ready to take on the world.

The number of homeless people—and families—is up in twenty-seven major U.S. cities. In New York City's shelter system alone the population of homeless singles is up from 10,223 to 10,978 from 1988 to 1989. The National Coalition for the Homeless estimates that there are twenty to twenty-four thousand homeless children in New York City alone. Approximately 10,000 of these are teenagers. Among the nation's tens of thousands of homeless teens, many are no longer under the guidance of parents. Within the spectrum of America's burgeoning population of homeless, this book focuses on the least communicative and most explosive group—teenagers.

We have not seen or heard enough from this volatile age group who are soon to join the ranks of America's adults. Teens feel an especially powerful peer pressure, and it is most difficult for them to admit that they don't have personal space of their own at a real address.

The young people you see and hear in this collection are exceptions. The initial subjects of this collection opened up only because they were being interviewed by their peers. Distrustful of social workers and guidance counselors, as well as reporters, these young people were nonetheless eager to share their stories with each other. When promised anonymity, they were enthusiastic about seeing their stories in print.

Many of the teenagers here were raised in homes with a substance abuser parent or were themselves enticed into the shadow world of drugs and alcohol. The subjects of these interviews seem frighteningly typical when one considers that three out of four Americans try an illegal drug before they reach twenty-five. Homelessness and substance abuse too often go hand in hand.

The young users and dealers are often bound for correctional facilities or prostitution dens where their lives are imperiled by complications like AIDS. With all we have read about the prevalence of AIDS, we were still shaken when several of these young people disclosed that they were carrying the deadly virus.

Broken homes, broken bodies and broken spirits have driven many of these kids to the streets, detention or rehab centers, prisons, or a series of group homes, foster homes, shelters or welfare hotels. The neglect and abuse of children by their parents and guardians that is recorded here is often staggering. Authorities estimate that as many as one out of every four girls and one of seven boys in this country is sexually abused or molested by age eighteen. A federal government report in the February 5, 1990, *New York Times* put the number of shelter youth that are sexually abused by family members at over sixty percent. Less than ten percent of the nation's sexual abuse ever gets reported.

The young victims of sexual, physical and emotional abuse too often turn against themselves. They are increasingly doing themselves in with more effective tools than a crack pipe. The suicide rate for the 15–24 age group is up 300 percent in the last thirty years.

Far too many of these teens have been torn from homes and have fallen into society's torn safety nets from cold circumstances beyond their parent's control. The shelters and welfare hotels are filled with the victims of unfair rent laws and greedy landlords. Thousands of hard-working low income families have been evicted from moderate rentals so that their apartments could be warehoused, refurbished and then rented out to young urban professions—for up to five times the original rent. Gentrification has not been all that gentle.

Whether it is the causes or effects of homelessness that one is exploring, there is no substitute for reading the faces and words of the subjects themselves.

Due to the many personal and legal areas of sensitivity, most identifying facts have been altered. Photos accompanying each monologue may be substitutes for the actual teens who are "speaking."

The subjects' responses were somewhat edited for clarity, but the language and content remain intact. Many slang terms are explained in a glossary at the back of the book. There was some self-censorship of what is ironically called "adult" language and "adult" situations; this to keep the book appropriate for younger readers and school libraries.

It is hoped that researchers young and old will find these monologues to be valuable sources of primary material about homelessness and also about the accompanying social problems listed in the index. These topics include AIDS, alcoholism, crime, domestic violence, drug abuse, prostitution, rape, sexual abuse, suicide, and teen pregnancy.

It is hoped, too, that parents and children who read these monologues do everything they can to prevent such tragedies from occurring in their own homes and communities.

I. E. Mozeson
New York City
1990

Angelique Garrety
16 years old

I was living with my mother and sister in a two-bedroom apartment in Canarsie when the building was sold. The new owner tripled the rent, and it was impossible for my mom to pay it. She had been working as a model, mainly for Sears, and her income was irregular. She tried to fight the landlord in small claims court, but she lost. One day we came home to find that the landlord had changed our locks. We were horrified. We couldn't even get into the apartment. We just didn't know where to go. We all spent that first night sleeping in a car. My mother acted completely helpless, and I was the one who had to get friends' houses to sleep in for the following night.

For a month we went from one friend's house to another, but we knew we couldn't continue like this. My mother finally went to the EAU and we were assigned to a shelter on Catherine Street. About half the people there were evicted from their previous homes for not paying rent. The worst part of living in a shelter was the lack of privacy. Also, there were fights all the time. A lot of the women living there were just plain crazy. And the kids from Smith, the projects across the street, were always looking for trouble. Fights broke out all the time between the Smith kids and the shelter kids. One of our security guards got into trouble for stabbing a kid from Smith. It was even in the papers.

Just the day I got registered in PS 131, after missing two months of school, we ran into trouble. You see, my mom had gotten into a fight with another woman. They had both been drinking, and the other woman demanded that my mother hand her some money from the welfare check my mother had just received. My mother refused, and this woman attacked my mother. But my mom was the one who got caught. The security guard saw my mom on top of this other woman, and it looked like my mother had started the fight. And so we had to leave the shelter on Catherine Street.

For the next two weeks we again went from one friend's house to another. Then one night we went back to the EAU and were assigned to the Bronx Park Motel. The Bronx Park Motel was nice enough, but we only stayed there a few days. Then we were told to go to the Prospect Hotel in the Bronx. That's where we've been for the last year.

It is terrible here, real shabby and dark. Crack, heroin, pills—you name it, and you'll find it here. There's an abandoned store across the street, and that's where everyone crawls through a hole to get their drugs. Every once in a while the cops clean the place out, but within a few days it's business as usual. There are even shootouts every now and then, but the dealers keep on returning. I can't wait to get out of here. I recently met a guy whom I really like, but I refuse to tell him where I live. It's too embarrassing, and I don't think he would understand. Maybe some day I'll tell him.

My parents separated when I was twelve years old. It amazes me that they stayed together as long as they did. They had absolutely nothing in common. They kept on breaking up and making up. This seemed to go on forever till my father finally found somebody new and moved out. My sister is now living with my father, but he refuses to have anything to do with me. Even now, two years later, he still won't talk to me.

If I've learnt anything from the past few years, it's to avoid my mother's mistakes. I will never let myself fall behind in rent. I won't squander my money and live from day to day the way my mom always did. My mother is so immature. Perhaps she'll straighten out one day when I move out.

Radames Adames
17 years old

I always had a violent temper. I guess I was born with it. For most of my life I was able to control it. But about two years ago I started getting into trouble. The first incident occurred on Easter Sunday. Me and my homeboys were riding the BMT train home from Coney Island. Some white dudes started staring at us. I asked them what they were looking at. One of them, with his arm around his girl, answered, "You, you dirty spic." I had to smash in both their faces. I mean, man, what was I supposed to do? I ended up being arrested for assault and spending the night in a cell underground at Union Square.

Once I had a record I should have been more careful. But I wasn't. About a month later I was walking with my girl on Third Street and First Avenue. This dude came over and started rapping to my girl. Now what was I to do? I hurt him real bad, and got arrested again. I spent the night locked up.

Then last spring, I was having trouble with one of the dudes from the Avenue. I didn't like the way he was staring at me. But I knew that if I hurt him, I'd be put away this time. So I had my boy beat him up. My boy cracked his jaw, fractured his skull, and broke his nose. But I was the one who got arrested. There was no way I could convince the cops that I was innocent. I hired my own lawyer and after handing over $7,000 to him to keep me out of jail, I was sentenced to six months at Rikers.

When I first arrived at Rikers, I was real scared. But I knew that I couldn't let anyone know how frightened I was. At the same time I was afraid to act too big. So I decided to just be myself. It worked for me.

Within an hour after my arrival I was given the "Rikers Test." This test, I later learned, is given to all new inmates. My sneakers were taken. If I had not been able to get them back, I would have been everyone's sucker for the rest of my stay at Rikers. I had to fight to get back my sneakers. But I got them back, and the word was out that I was no sucker to be messed with. No one was going to take advantage of me.

Every day of my six months at Rikers—except for the twenty-one days I spent in solitary—was the same routine. We were awakened every morning at 7 o'clock by the guards' banging on our cell. From 8:00 to 2:00 we attended school. Now that was a joke for most of the guys. When they were out on the streets, they never went to school. So how the hell were they supposed to care now that they were in jail? Most of the dudes just kept their heads down on their desks and slept. When they weren't asleep, they'd be fighting. Fights broke out all the time. I kinda felt sorry for the teachers. Many of them were there because they wanted to help us. But they were really boring, and we dissed them all the time. And one of them got really hurt. She got caught in the middle of a fight between two dudes and got hit in her eye. I think she had to lose her eye.

The day really started after school ended. By about 4:00 we'd all be zooted. Drugs were always available. They were smuggled in by our girlfriends. When a girl would come to visit her man, she'd store the drugs in little balloons in her bra. Then she'd ask to go the bathroom, where she transferred these balloons to her mouth. When she saw her guy, she'd start to make out with him and during their kissing, the drug-filled balloons would get transferred into the guy's mouth. He swallowed then as quickly as possible. And, as you know, what goes in one end comes out the other. So that's how most of the drugs got into Rikers.

Besides cheeba, the most popular drug was mescaline. We'd mix the shit with toothpaste and roll it up in cigarette papers. It looked as though we were smoking cigarettes. But mescaline is chill. It is an eight-hour high. There was plenty of coke available, too. This was mostly supplied by the guards. A half a gram went for $40, but we often gave the guards all kinds of other stuff like food and jewelry in exchange for the coke. These guards were mostly Black Muslims and were supposed to be laying off drugs and certainly not dealing them. But that wasn't what was happening.

When we weren't getting high, we'd be play-fighting. But just about every day these play fights turned into real fights. There were a lot of dead bodies removed from Rikers during the six months I was there. Lots of guys got chopped up. We'd be fighting each other and the guards would be reading the papers. Every morning when I woke up, I prayed hard to God that I'd live through the day.

Now at Rikers you either take care of others in your cell or you are taken care of. You either protect or find someone to protect you. I had nine sons. I quickly became known as "Body Guard." That's the name that everybody at Rikers knows me by. Almost no one there knows my real name. My sons gave me their money—we called it rent money—and I protected them. Nobody, and I mean nobody, messed with my sons. A few times I was written up for extortion, but what the hell. I was living high. I ate the best food and had about twenty pairs of sneakers.

I even took care of some dudes who weren't my sons. The Black guys had no respect for each other. They always messed each other up. But we Puerto Ricans tried to help each other. The first time you take a shower at Rikers, the dudes who've been there for awhile check you over. If you look easy, they'll finish you off. I always protected my Spanish brothers. But if a Black dude was getting it in the ass, I'd just chill and enjoy the scene. And these little dudes would be crying, man. They'd be terrified.

The whole time I was at Rikers I only saw one white dude. He was pathetic. We stole everything from him and had him doing our laundry. One day the guard pulled him out of his cell to tell him that he got a phone call. We knew something was up. People don't be getting phone calls like that at Rikers. Anyway, his mom had just died. She overdosed. This poor white dude couldn't stop crying. I felt so sorry for him that I let him stay with me that one day.

I had one real bad time at Rikers—the 21 days I was in solitary. Some big Black dude tried to take over my sons. And I had to mess him up. He needed seventy-five stitches by the time I finished with him. And I got thrown into solitary. Now that is hell. Not once was I allowed to take a shower. I wasn't allowed to buy food from the commissary, so I was stuck with the food the inmates made. The guards would come by and throw the food into my cell. But since there was no way I was going to drink kool-aid that was pissed in or eat cereal mixed with snot, I almost starved to death. By day eighteen of solitary, I thought I had lost my mind. All I did was scream and cry. Now it's just one bad memory.

Most of my six months at Rikers I was living high. I did more stealing, more getting high and more fighting than I'd done in my entire life. But I also managed to get my GED. I never would've gotten my diploma if I hadn't been forced to attend school. I was just released last week, and I'm trying now to enroll in college in time for the spring semester.

Anita Santos
18 years old

I was fourteen years old. My mother had gone down to Puerto Rico to visit her mother. I was sitting on the couch in the living room watching *The Honeymooners*. It was about midnight. Suddenly my stepfather started looking at me funny. He offered me a drink, but I refused to take it. My stepfather went over to the T.V. and turned it off. Before I knew what was happening, he had pulled me down and was holding me too hard. I had never liked the way he touched me, but this was the first time he had forced himself on me.

I was short and chubby, and had never had a boyfriend. But my stepfather wanted me anyway. I didn't know what to do. I fell on the floor dragging the plant on the coffee table with me. My stepfather slapped me and raped me. He took away my virginity. I hated him. I just wanted to kill him.

I began to cry uncontrollably. I felt dizzy and almost fainted. I was trembling. I wanted to scream, but I didn't. I was afraid that my brother and sister who were asleep in the next room would wake up and find out what had happened. I kept on hoping that my mother would suddenly return and murder him. I attacked the skinny, smelly wimp and bit him. He was bleeding. He started to run after me with a knife. I thought he was going to kill me. I managed to escape. I ran straight into my cousin's apartment on the next block.

Two days later, my mother returned from Puerto Rico. I called her from my cousin's house. As soon as she came over, I told her what had happened. She refused to believe me. She said that I'd always hated my stepfather and was imagining things. She said I hated him because I couldn't forgive him for taking my father's place. My real father had died when I was six years old. She started crying. She couldn't stop. But her tears meant nothing to me. I hated her for not believing me. I told her that there was no way I was ever going back home as long as my stepfather was there. She told me that she couldn't live without my stepfather. Besides, she was sure that I was imagining things. She didn't know what to do with me. So she decided to take me to the psychiatric ward at Bellevue.

I stayed at Bellevue for a month. It was a crazy house. All these big people were being put in straitjackets all the time. I felt that I didn't belong there. If anyone in my family was crazy, it was my mother and stepfather. There was one social worker who was real kind. But every time I told her what had happened to me, she started crying. She was pregnant, and I felt sorry for her. I started feeling guilty for making her cry. I also became real friendly with one of the interns whom I'm now dating. It seemed that everyone had believed me except for my own mother.

After I spent a month at Bellevue, my mother tried to convince me to return home. But there was no way I ever would unless she got rid of my stepfather. So I was sent to a group home in Westchester. I liked it there. I sang in the local church chorus. I was real smart in school. The only thing that bothered me were the fights between some of the girls in the other cottages. But in my cottage things were pretty cool.

After I graduated high school, which was two years ago, I had to leave the home. I wasn't prepared to live alone, so I tried living with my aunt uptown. But I couldn't stand it. Her kids were all dealing drugs, and here I was going to college trying to get my life together. After her apartment was raided, I knew I had to find another living arrangement.

So for the past year I've been living by myself in my grandmother's apartment on the F.D.R. Drive. My grandmother's in Puerto Rico, and she lives there most of the year. I try to have as little to do with my mother as possible, and I never see my stepfather. I've been hearing from my brother how my stepfather has started beating my mother. My mother was just diagnosed as having breast cancer, but she refuses to go for chemotherapy. She doesn't want to lose her hair. She tells me if it's her time to go, then she's ready. She's forty-one years old.

I never understood why my mother stays with my stepfather. My mother has a good job working as a county clerk and she makes enough money to support our family. My stepfather works at the post office, and he earns $700 a week, but he never contributes to the family's expenses. He spends all his money gambling. Also, he's unfaithful to my mother. My brother tells me that last year he was having an affair with a nineteen-year old slut who lives in their building. When my mother confronted the little bitch, my father beat up my mother. He doesn't care that she's dying. In fact, he told her that he's waiting for her to die.

My mother just wrote her will. And would you believe that she's leaving most of her money to my stepfather? I guess they deserve each other.

As for me, after I graduate college, I plan to go to law school. I'd like to become a lawyer and help other rape victims.

Dave Frank
22 years old

I was thrown out by my real parents when I was three. I didn't meet them again until I was eighteen. According to my records— 'cause I can't keep track of all this—I was in fourteen foster homes all over Pennsylvania between ages three and seven. At seven I was officially adopted into a family that had seventeen adopted kids. Yeh, even my one family was an institution.

My adoptive father was a psychologist. He said I was emotionally disturbed and had me in and out of state facilities where he worked. I got in trouble when I was eighteen. One of my adoptive brothers and I were pretty close. He started a fire and burned down a whole warehouse. No one was hurt, but the charges were serious. My brother had a record and they would have put him away for many years. So I went and said I did it. I took the rap because it was only my first offense.

They still sent me to prison. I served a whole year and a half. My brother only avoided me after that. He couldn't look me in the eye from guilt or something.

My adoptive father got investigated by the state for sexually abusing boys under his care. When they asked me in court if I was ever abused by him, I said, "Yes." My father would tell us that we owed him. He'd tell us, "I'm your father. This is the closest a father could get."

I knew that some of my other adoptive brothers were sexually abused too, but only one of them was ready to talk. Our testimony got dismissed because there was a two-year statute of limitations on those cases. Dad was very smooth at the trial. He "proved" that we were psychologically unfit to give testimony; he got acquitted even though six boys in all spoke up for the prosecution.

His rep was ruined, though, and half the state of Pennsylvania wanted to lynch him. He moved to somewhere in the Midwest with his loyal little wife, my adoptive Mom.

Years later when a newspaper was writing me up as a crime victim, a reporter investigated my story and found out that my father got himself a job as a director of an institute for adolescent boys. I was pretty angry. I knew how he worked. He had only adopted me and my brothers because he had access to our files and knew we were written up for problems of sexual identity. My sisters were only adopted so it wouldn't look too suspicious.

I got a hold of the institute where he was working. I called them and told them about everything that went on in Pennsylvania and with me. They confirmed everything and launched an investigation. Meanwhile, I got my parent's home number

and called it. My mom answered. I said, "Hi Mom, it's David."
There was silence. Then she said, "Don't you ever call here
again" and hung up.

I was finished with my home town. I just went to the bus
station one day to see where my little life savings could take me.
I found out that I had a few more dollars than it took to get to
New York, so I got on the bus. I came to the city with nothing
and quickly learned to sell myself for spending money. I kept to
the bus station area; it was the only place I got to know at first.
I got one serious lover, but he was pretty abusive. We lived in
hotels across from the Holland, with all the welfare people. I
sold some crack too. I didn't use the stuff. I couldn't afford it.

I haven't had an address in years. I live in Riverside Park
most of the time and go into the tunnels beneath the park when
the weather's bad. There are old Amtrak tunnels in different
parts of town that are underground cities. They have their own
mayors and everything. In the salt mines near the piers the boss
is called the president. The mines are big salt sheds used to
salt city streets in the winter. I lived there for a few months
too. Some reporter wrote it up, so the city came and closed
it—probably because we were mostly gay men.

We weren't violent, but we did commit a lot of unreported
robberies. We'd set up gay johns from out-of-town and shake
them down. I never did any of the robbing, but I was often one
of the lookouts. I was the victim of violence myself. We were
beaten up in a gay-bashing incident uptown that got plenty of
media attention. My friend was almost killed in the stabbing attack, and I was badly beaten. That's when the reporters came to
talk to me. It was the first time anyone wanted to hear my story.

One of those reporters tracked down my adoptive father in the Midwest, and you know what I did with that information.

The reporter also got into files that allowed me to look up my birth parents. I found out that I was illegitimate and that my mother is practically a hooker. My birth father is a constable in a small Pennsylvania town. His latest common-law wife is eighteen, younger than me. When we contacted them, they didn't want anything to do with me. They say that blood is thicker than water. Don't believe it!

I think I would have been gay even if I wasn't abused. At seven I already had feelings. My adoptive father just speeded things along. I was never real open about gayness until that gay-bashing attack. Instead of getting scared, I got angry. Now I'm ready to talk about being gay and being abused. I don't want other kids like me thinking that they are the only ones in the world with these problems.

I have leukemia, and the doctors don't give me more than two or three years. I really don't think about it. I'm busy looking for my next meal. The Crime Victims' Board is trying to get me more money, to prove a doctor's claim that my leukemia was brought on by my getting beaten unconscious. I get chemotherapy every Wednesday—when I show up. I'll know in a couple of weeks if they will be amputating my right foot.

Stacey Ortiz Carron
15 years old

Since the age of eight, I've spent most of my life in and out of shelters and welfare hotels. There's me, my dad, my three brothers and my two sisters. My mother abandoned us when I was four years old. I know that she had emotional problems and was not able to take care of us. I don't blame her, although there were many times that I wished she was there for me.

My dad tried to keep the family together. It was very hard for him to raise six children on his own. He really couldn't work, and we were living on welfare. Our biggest problem was staying in one place. Things never seemed to work out.

In fact, I think I've been in every shelter in New York City. When we weren't in shelters or welfare hotels, we were living in apartments that were worse than holes. But we usually ended up being evicted from these apartments. Or they burnt down. My father's now in jail because they say he burnt down the last apartment we were living in. I don't know if he did. But I do know he was having trouble with the landlady. She had accused my father of sexually abusing me. She was a real witch.

Things had gotten so bad with her that at one point we were sleeping in Grand Central Station because we were afraid to return to the apartment. This landlady was recently in the newspapers. It seems she was thrown into jail for doing a lot of illegal stuff with the apartment buildings she owned. But she was soon bailed out. At least, that's what I heard.

The worst part of all the fires in the apartments, or holes, that we lived in was losing all my awards and trophies. You see, no matter what was going on in my life and regardless of how many different schools I had to transfer to, I've always been a good student. I'm determined not to let all the crap pull me down. I know I'm gonna make it no matter what. This is my vengeance. I know I am as good as anyone else. And nothing is gonna stop me. I can't give up, 'cause that's what people want.

There really wasn't much of a difference between the apartments and shelters we were living in. None of them was safe. Maybe Grand Central Station was the safest place I ever slept in. But the worst had to be the Martinique Hotel. Me, my two sisters, my three brothers and my father were given two tiny rooms and a hot plate. I was so scared there that I couldn't even sleep at night. There were fires almost every day. And everything was stolen from us. Even my sister's underpants. Can you imagine somebody wanting her underpants? Just about everyone was either selling drugs or doing drugs there, even the security. One of the thugs there put a loaded gun to my younger brother's head. When I complained to one of the cops, he just said to me, "If any bastard bothers you, just slash him."

I came home one day from school to the Martinique to find out that my father was put in jail. My older sister was crying. We didn't know what to do. I hooked up with a social worker from Special Services for Children and she sent me to a group home on University Avenue in the Bronx. I stayed there for four months. I shared my room with another girl. The home itself wasn't bad and the girls were pretty nice. A lot of them were pregnant. The neighborhood, though, was terrible. Drug dealers were everywhere, and I was really afraid to walk down the block. I had to leave for school at 5:30 in the morning to get to Seward on time, and University Avenue is no place to be walking that early in the morning. So after four months, I was transferred to Shalimar, a group home in Lefrak City. It was pretty cool, except for one of the workers. I used to get into arguments with him. I heard that he was dealing.

One night when I was coming home late, I saw a whole bunch of TV cameras outside my building. I kept on asking people what was happening. Finally, I found out that there was a fire on my floor. Two of the workers were killed, including the guy I used to argue with. I was in a state of shock. Again, everything I owned was destroyed, including all my family pictures and the awards I'd just gotten.

Now I'm living in another group home in Lefrak City. It's okay and I expect to be here for awhile. There are ten girls all together between the ages of thirteen to fifteen. Most of the girls live two in a room. But since I've been real good, I have my own room. And since I'm on level five, the highest level you can earn, I have an 11 o'clock curfew.

When people ask me where I live, I tell them that I live in an apartment in Queens. I really don't want people to know my business. I'm afraid they'd look down on me. I don't think most people could understand everything I've been through.

Carmen Mendez
16 years old

I never knew my mother. I think she was about seventeen when I was born. My dad decided that he would raise me on his own. He tried to be a good father. But when I was about five years old, he started to leave me alone. It was very scary. I did not like being left alone in the apartment. The most frightening time was when there was a fire in the building. The firemen came and all the other tenants left the building. I spent the whole time I hiding out in the bathroom. I'm lucky to be alive.

When I was about ten years old, my father started acting moody. I think he was having girlfriend problems. One night he tried to kill himself. I didn't know what to do. There really wasn't anybody I could talk to. Nothing I ever did pleased him. Then, when I was eleven years old, my father came into bed with me one night and started doing strange things. It was horrible.

Two years later, he married this lady. I hated my stepmother. She blamed me for every problem she had with my father. She had me doing all the housework. One night, when I didn't feel like going to the supermarket, she told my father to choose between her and me. Later that evening, I tried to kill myself. I swallowed a whole bottle of my stepmother's Valium.

When my father found me unconscious, he rushed me to the Emergency Room at Beth Israel Hospital. I spent two and a half weeks recovering at Beth Israel. Then I was sent to a diagnostic center behind the hospital. I met some people who cared, and I started talking to them about my problems. I never again saw my former home on Avenue D. The social workers would not allow me to return home. My father was told that he could not see me unless he agreed to go into therapy. He refused, and it's now been three years since I've seen my dad. I suppose I still love him. I guess you always love your father, but if I never saw him again, it would be fine with me.

For the past two years I have been living in a group home in East Harlem. There are two kids in each room and nine other kids all together. When I first got here, I was very frightened. I was afraid the girls would hate me, even jump me.

But I'm happier than I've ever been. I'm never blamed for things that I didn't do. If there's a problem, we all sit down and work it out. I also met a girl who is now my best friend. I spend weekends with her when she visits her mother. We love each other like sisters. There are five ladies and one man who are in charge of our home. I like them all, but Mrs. Green is my favorite. She is like the mother that I never had.

I am given respect and independence here. I even have a clothes allowance and can choose my own wardrobe. We have an 11 o'clock curfew, and we all try to keep it. I only broke it once, and then I was given some extra chores to do around the house. I can invite friends over. If someone doesn't want to be my friend because I live in a group home, then tough on them. I don't need those kinds of friends.

Someday I would like to move to Puerto Rico. Maybe I could find my real mother there. I know that one day when I have children, I will always be there for them.

Alfonzo Rivera
17 years old

I lived most of my life in a three-bedroom apartment on Rodger Street in Brooklyn. About five years ago we started having trouble with the landlord. You see, my older brother is retarded. He wasn't born that way. But when he was about two years old, he started eating the plaster off the walls in our apartment. Before my mother even knew what was happening, the doctor told her that my brother was brain damaged. It seems that the plaster he had been eating destroyed his brain cells.

As my brother got older, he became more and more difficult. When he couldn't get his way, he would throw violent tantrums.

He always wanted to blast his music. Neighbors were constantly complaining. My mother didn't know what to do and she didn't want to put my brother away.

One day I came home from junior high school to find out that we had been evicted. My brother had gone after one of the neighbors with a butcher knife. The landlord called the cops and we were told to leave or face charges.

My mother fell apart. She didn't know what to do. My father was living in Puerto Rico, and my mother didn't even know how to reach him. She put my brother into Kings County hospital and me, my mom, and my two sisters moved into my aunt's apartment on the F.D.R.

We stayed there for about four months. But things didn't work out. Now my mom and aunt aren't even talking to each other. It was too crowded there with my aunt, her boyfriend, my two cousins and my family. And we kept on getting on each other's nerves.

My aunt then helped my mother get us into the shelter on Catherine Street. I hated Catherine Street. We were put into a small room with another family. We didn't even have our own bathroom. I was so embarrassed to be in a shelter that I never told anyone where I was living. I broke up with my girlfriend, because I was afraid she'd find out. I kept on going to school every day. Then I got a job after school just to have some place to go. I tried to spend as little time as possible at Catherine.

Six months later we were moved to a welfare hotel in Brooklyn. There at least we had our own bathroom. But me, my mom, and my two sisters were stuck in one tiny room. Also, there were too many people selling drugs. Drugs aren't my thing. I have my rap music to get me high. Just give me Kool Moe Dee or M.C. Lyte. But I worried about my younger sisters. We were stuck in the hotel for six months.

Finally, the city found an apartment for us in these projects in East New York. These projects have got to be more dangerous

than the shelter or the hotel. Everyone—and I mean everyone—
here is dealing drugs. The first week we moved in a gun was put
to my head and all my jewelry was stolen. We're afraid to ride
in the elevators because people are held up all the time. But, at
least, my brother is back with us and our family is all together in
our own place.

Vanessa Brooks
15 years old

I grew up in a two-bedroom apartment on East 222nd Street in the Bronx. Two years ago, the building was sold, and the landlord more than tripled the rent to $800 a month. Within a month, my mother, me and my two sisters had no place to live. First we went to my aunt's house. But her apartment is small and she has three sons, so there really wasn't enough room for us. A month later, we tried living with my godmother, but my mother didn't want to have to depend on the good will of other people for shelter. So, about six weeks later, we went to the EAU office in the Bronx. We stayed there for eight hours until we were finally assigned to a shelter on Catherine Street.

When we first arrived at the shelter, we were scared. We didn't know anyone, and we didn't know what to expect. But one of the security guards befriended us, and we began to feel more comfortable. My mom was working as a nurse for the V.A., and me and my sisters went to school every day. So we spent as little time as possible at the shelter. I was glad to go to school just to get out of the shelter. I didn't even eat breakfast there. Breakfast consisted of powdered eggs or some starchy pancakes, so we usually ended up buying our food at the corner grocery store.

The most difficult thing about living in Catherine was the lack of privacy. Also, I really missed my mother's cooking. My family kept to ourselves, so we really didn't get involved in any of the fighting or drug dealing that went on there. I never told anyone where I was living. It was too embarrassing.

Since our stay there was not supposed to be more than twenty-one days, every few weeks a van would pick us up to take us somewhere else. About a month after we'd arrived at Catherine, we were taken to the Golden Gate, a hotel in Sheepshead Bay. We really liked it there, but the owner decided that shelter people weren't welcome, so two weeks later we had to leave. We then returned to the EAU who sent us back to Catherine Street. A month later, we were sent to the Prince George Hotel. It was terrible there. There were drug addicts everywhere, and, instead of going to school, the hotel kids hung out in the streets robbing people. My mom complained, and we returned to Catherine Street. A few weeks later, we were sent in a van to the Martinique. As we arrived there, firecrackers were hurled at the van. So my mother refused to even leave the van.

We returned to Catherine, where we spent most of the past year. Since my mother was not on welfare, she was not getting the help finding an apartment that most of the welfare recipients got. And so we were stuck. About two months ago, my mother hurt her knee and was eligible for disability payments. Finally, we got help finding an apartment. And just last week we moved into our own two-bedroom apartment in Eastchester Gardens on Gunhill Road. We were so happy to have our own place, that we didn't even mind sleeping on the wooden floor of an empty apartment our first night there.

I don't blame my mother for what we went through. If it was anyone's fault, it was my father's for cutting out on us and leaving us no money. He had a lot of money, but we never saw any of it. The woman he hooked up with after he left us poisoned him and took all of his money. After my father died, she left town. We are still trying to locate the children whom my father had with this woman. I don't know if we ever will. I hear that their son looks just like me.

Shaundese Green
15 years old

I couldn't stand listening to my mother and stepfather's constant arguing. And staying in the apartment was so boring. So I got in with a crowd that hung out all night, and soon I was dealing drugs.

Money had always been a problem. My mother was very stingy with my allowance, and I never had enough money for clothes or tapes or any of the stuff a teenager needs. Selling drugs seemed like the answer to my problems. It got me out of my apartment and earned me all the money I needed.

I started hanging out later and later, and my mother and stepfather starting arguing more and more. One evening, my mom found some cocaine under my mattress. She decided then that she didn't want me living at home any more. I guess that she felt I was a bad influence on my younger brother and sister. She also felt that I was driving her and my stepfather apart.

She took me to the Teen Center in downtown Brooklyn and just left me there. I felt awful. I was told that I had to stay there until a permanent placement was found for me.

At the Teen Center there were two girls to a room. I could hardly sleep the first night I was there. The girls were nasty, and the mattresses were filthy. The whole place was unsanitary. Nobody searches you when you come in, so people bring in guns, knives, crack and weed. The girls try to impress you by sticking a gun to your head if you give them any trouble.

The staff at the Teen Center is nice, though. They try to make you feel comfortable. In the morning we had school. Every afternoon we had rap sessions, and then we were given chores to do. We'd sweep, vacuum, or clean the bathrooms. At the end of each day we were paid for the work we did. Sometimes we were taken on trips. We got to see a lot of movies.

Finally, after about three months of staying at the Teen Center, the social workers decided to send me to Lakeside, a detention home or lock-up in upstate New York. It was terrible there. We slept four in a room. Not a day went by without a serious fight. My things got stolen all the time. Even my favorite tape was stolen. One day all my make-up was emptied all over my bed for no reason. I screamed, "Which bitch did this?" and I went straight for the nearest girl in sight. But I ended up breaking my own dresser. If the girls didn't like the way you looked, or if they were jealous of you for any reason, you were in serious danger.

We got paid at the end of every week for whatever chores we did that week. There was one girl there, Leticia, who kept on making more money than the rest of us. One Friday she had earned twenty-six dollars. Plus she had thirty-two of her own.

Just as she was getting ready to go to the flea market to buy some relaxer for her hair, a whole bunch of girls jumped her to get her money. She ended up getting all sliced up. The cops were called and an ambulance had to come.

Eventually, I was transferred to the Shalimar Group Home in Lefrak City. The girls there were real tough. If you didn't like your placement, you would purposely act bad. That way the social workers would be forced to change your placement. So on many days the girls would purposely get drunk and act rowdy. Then they'd fight or jump somebody, so that they'd be thrown out and put in another home. At Shalimar I saw a twelve-year-old girl get beaten up real bad for no reason by a group of drunk girls. The girls thought they were having fun.

I've been back home with my mother and stepfather now since the summer. I really don't do much all day. I spend most of the day watching the soaps on T.V. and I chill. I know that if I want to stay out of trouble, I've gotta stay out of the streets. Everybody comes up here to the Heights to buy drugs,—they come in from New Jersey, Connecticut, Long Island—and the temptation to deal is too great. I don't ever want to be sent away again. Despite the problems in my family, I don't ever want to go back to any other home. One of these days soon I'm gonna try to get enrolled in high school and see what I can do with my life.

David Diaz
17 years old

I had expected to spend last summer in Puerto Rico with my grandmother. Instead, I ended up at Rikers.

I was hanging out at Sheriff Park with kids I'd known all my life. For the past three years, since we were about fourteen, we'd stay out every night till, like, four in the morning. We usually just smoked weed and drank beer. When we drank a lot of beer, we'd sometimes get a little rowdy. About two years ago, I was picked up for disorderly conduct and kept overnight in the housing police station.

My mother was so angry. She's a real straight lady with a good job in computers. She always worried about me when I stayed out late. She didn't know what to do with me, and she was afraid I'd end up like my cousin who's been in and out of Rikers the past six years for selling drugs. So my mother sent me to Park Slope to live with my father.

I couldn't stand living with him. He was just as strict as my mother. But what made it worse was his attitude. You see he's got this attitude that he knows it all. That's why my mother left him when I was eight years old. He always has to be right. He never makes mistakes. He's the perfect one. But my father couldn't control me either. I used to take the train to Delancey Street and break night with my homeboys in Sheriff Park.

So, after one summer of living with my father, I was back home with my mother. Things weren't that good. I continued hanging out late and my mother was always on my back. She was afraid I was going to get into trouble again. She was planning to send me to Puerto Rico to live with my grandmother.

Right before I was supposed to leave for Puerto Rico, me and my homeboys started having some beef with some older guys from the Avenue. One hot night one of them came with his posse. As one of the dudes started to approach me, I grabbed my bat and hit him over the head. I broke his nose and messed up his head. Before I knew what was happening, I was arrested on an attempted murder charge.

I was sent to the bull pen on Centre Street. For three days I was stuck with thirty smelly guys in one room. It had one long bench around its four sides and you had to fight for your spot. There was one toilet. The whole place stank. I knew some of the guys from the Avenue who were picked up for dealing drugs and stealing cars. I was real scared and just tried to chill. It was like a bad dream.

After three days, I was sent to Rikers. I was put into a cell with three other guys. Two of them were in for robbery. One of them was picked up for selling drugs to an undercover.

My first day there, three hard rocks came over to me and took my sneakers and my gold chain. They asked me for them. I just kept my head down and gave over my stuff. I wasn't gonna fight for things I could replace when I felt that my life was in danger. But for the next month, everyone took advantage of me. I started to feel like a real sucker. When I finally decided to strike back, the guard caught me.

I spent two days in solitary, but each hour felt like six. You can't imagine what it's like to be in a room with four walls and nothing to do but stare at them. But at least I was safe in solitary. After I was taken out of solitary, I just kept to myself and tried to stay out of trouble. I would have liked to go to the gym and work out. But too many fights broke out all the time. If you tried to change the weights, the guy who'd been using them before you was ready to fight you. So I stayed out of the gym.

During the two months I spent at Rikers I didn't see even one white inmate. All the dudes were either Black or Spanish. The real hard rocks were mostly Black. I don't think they should send a white dude to Rikers. I don't think he'd survive.

By the end of August, my mother had hired a private lawyer for me. She was real worried about me, and someone in her office knew somebody who was able to help me out. At my trial, all charges against me were dismissed. It was proven that I had acted in self-defense. I did. I never would have hit somebody over the head for no reason.

But now that I know what Rikers is like, I know I have to keep out of trouble, any kind of trouble. So I've been spending most of my time just by myself. And that's just how it's gonna be for a while.

Sonia Lucas
14 years old

It's been three years since we had to leave our apartment on the Upper West Side. I'm not too sure why we left. I think it's because my mother was evicted when she couldn't afford to pay the rent.

For the past three years, I've been living with my mother, my twelve-year-old sister, and my little brother in a welfare hotel in the South Bronx. I hate it here. I never tell anybody where I live. I never let any of my friends walk me home, and I swore my best friend—who I met here—to secrecy.

Things have been real rough. My mom spends most of her time on the corner dealing crack, but she never has any money. I don't think she does any crack, so I really don't know where her money goes. I think she gives it all to her boyfriend. He came here from Colombia a few years ago, and he supplies her with the stuff that she sells.

My mother disappears for days at a time, leaving me alone with my sister and little brother. My brother is six years old, but my mother never registered him in school. He spends most of the day in the room watching T.V.

As for me, I really haven't been going to school since we moved here. When we first moved here, I continued to go to my elementary school in Manhattan, but it was too far away. My guidance counselor transferred me to a junior high school in this neighborhood. I tried going a few times, but I kept on getting into fights with the girls there. I had one really bad fight about a year and a half ago. I didn't like the way one of the girls was looking at me, and things kind of got out of hand. I haven't been back since.

What's hardest on me is that I feel that my mother has put me in charge of the family. I'm the one who always has to take care of my younger sister and brother. Sometimes I feel as though I'm the one who gave birth to them. My mother is also on my back to keep the apartment in order. She expects me to make sure there is food in the apartment, but she never gives me any money. So I have to babysit in order to support the family. Once I had to pawn my favorite ring for thirty dollars just to get milk and bread into the house. When my mother found out that my ring was missing (I told her I lost it), she beat me up. She kept on screaming, "You're so careless. Can't you take care of anything?"

My mother never believes me, so there's really no point in ever telling her the truth. What really gets me is that she expects me to hand over all my baby-sitting money to her. How does she expect me to feed the kids? I wish my mother would grow up and assume some responsibility. She's forty-two years old.

Even though life has been real rough the last few years, I'm never tempted to get high. I don't even drink. That's a real cop-out. Life here has taught me to assume responsibility. My situation has probably made me stronger.

There's talk these days of closing down this hotel. I can't wait. Once we get our own apartment, I am going back to school. I sure don't want to end up like my mom.

Lisa Cabrera
15 years old

My earliest memory of my mother is of her drinking a bottle of Clorox in front of me. I was four years old. I remember her telling me that she was drinking that poison because she wanted to die. I remember crying, "Please, Mommy, don't." The next thing I remember is my father calling an ambulance and my mother being rushed to the emergency room.

When I was five years old, my father was sent to Rikers for dealing drugs. My mother felt that she couldn't go on without him. She was only fifteen years old when I was born and she was very dependent upon him. She tried to slit her wrists. I still remember all the blood.

Then my mother was sent to some rest home upstate. She stayed there for a year and a half while I lived with my grandmother. My aunt had tried to get custody of me, but it was decided that I'd stay with my grandma until my mother was well again.

When I was seven years old, my mother came back home and moved in with me and my grandmother. Within a few months, she hooked up with my stepfather. He was a young handsome Italian guy who owned his own hardware store. We moved in with him, and for a while things were okay. My mother was even working. She was helping sell appliances in the store.

When I was nine years old, my mother became pregnant, but the baby died when she was two days old. I can't believe that I once had a sister. I wish I did now. Anyway, after the baby died, my mother got real depressed again. That's when she started messing around with drugs.

I blame my stepfather. He used to snort cocaine occasionally, but soon he and my mother were shooting up all the time. They were mixing all kinds of drugs: heroin, cocaine, speed. And they were sharing needles. Then about five years ago, my stepfather was diagnosed as having the AIDS virus. He died a year later when my mother was pregnant with my brother. My mother did not know that she had AIDS nor that my brother would be born with AIDS.

My mother was okay until about two years ago. She started feeling sick alot, and started spending a lot of time in the hospital. At that point, my baby brother went to live with my grandmother and I went to live with my aunt.

My mother just died two months ago. Her last year was terrible. She could hardly breathe, could barely walk and spent most of the time in the intensive care unit at Bellevue Hospital. She had completely lost her will to live. I was afraid she'd kill herself before she died a natural death. But on the last day of her life, she was joking around. She told me that she knew her time was up. She had just seen her entire life flash before her eyes. I miss my mother so much. I still can't believe she's gone.

I feel so alone. I worry all the time about my brother. He's four years old and a real playful, healthy kid. But he's carrying the AIDS virus, and I know that at any time, he could get sick and die. Every time I see him, I get depressed. I keep on imagining him in his coffin. Now that's no way to see your brother. I also feel guilty that I can't help him or my grandmother. But there's really nothing I can do, but keep on living for me. It's a constant struggle for survival, even when you're not dying of AIDS.

Bobby Ramirez
17 years old

When I was thirteen years old, I fell in love with cocaine. My best friend at the time was Domingo. Domingo's mother, Anna, was a big time coke dealer. She had become a dealer to support her own habit, and she made loads of money. Whenever Domingo wanted any cocaine, all he had to do was ask his mom. I had started smoking marijuana when I was eleven, but I'd never done any coke. One day, though, I got curious. I told Anna that I wanted to try some coke. "No problem," she said. "Anything for Domingo's best friend."

Soon Anna was supplying me with one gram a day, and two grams on Saturdays and Sundays. She never took any money from me. The street value of the cocaine that I was snorting was about a thousand dollars a week. But for me it was free.

Anyway, after about a year and a half of this, my mom got suspicious. I hadn't been spending much time in school. I was in Wagner Jr. High School at the time. Instead of going to school all I did was hang out with Domingo, snort coke, and go to rock concerts. One morning when my mom was doing my laundry, she discovered some cocaine in my pants pocket. She freaked out. To this day she does not know that Anna was supplying me. Anna was doing me a favor, and I would never turn her in. Well, my mom called up some drug abuse hot line, and, after dozens of phone calls, she and my dad drove me upstate to Middletown Hospital.

They took me up to the second floor. I spent one week there being detoxified. That was the worst week of my life. When I wasn't unconscious, I was in terrible pain. My nose couldn't stop bleeding. I still have a hole in my nose from all the cocaine that I snorted.

I thought I would be going home after spending a week at Middletown. But my parents had other plans for me. My older brother told me that they were planning to put me in a drug rehab center in Port Jarvis, New York. I was real pissed and made plans to run away. All I could think about were the great tickets Domingo and I had for the Iron Maiden concert coming up that Sunday at Madison Square Garden. There was no way in the world I was going to miss that. Running away, though, was not possible. I had no money. I couldn't even afford a bus ticket out of there.

So I ended up going straight from the hospital to a huge home in the country. Riverside House was a private rehab center for drug addicts. Most of the guys there were older than me, and almost everyone there was Italian. My mom is Jewish and my dad is Puerto Rican, and I had hardly ever hung out with

Italians. Almost all my friends are Spanish. I hated the place at first. I was scared, and being out of the city freaked me out. My roommate, Pat, came off as a rich spoiled white boy. All that I knew about him was that his dad was a lawyer. For the first few days, I kept on plotting schemes to escape.

But the people at Riverside were too hip. They could read us junkies through and through. You see, everyone there including the cook, had been a drug addict. There was no way to "get over."

As the weeks became months, I began to love Riverside. It was home to me. In fact, it was better than home. At home my parents were always fighting. They were even legally divorced ten years ago, but continued to live together "for the sake of the kids." My mother has a boyfriend, a rich Black cowboy, who spends a lot of time in our house, even with my father around. And I never felt right about that. Also, my mom was always on my back about something or another. So now, for the first time in my life, I lived in a home where people treated each other with love and respect.

Also, I felt that I was needed. We were all given different jobs to help out around the house. We worked in the fields, chopped wood and took responsibility for one another's tasks. In fact, I personally became responsible for this guy Mike, who was crippled from the neck down. Mike had been in a car accident when he was high. He had survived the accident, but he was now stuck in a wheelchair for the rest of his life. He was a few years older than me and had been living at Riverside for four years. I helped Mike get dressed and undressed every day.

Back home on 28th Street, I had no way to release my anger. Here at Riverside there were boxing bags and basketball courts and constant ways to work out my frustration.

We met in groups three times a day. Each meeting went on for about two hours. We talked about our problems and what got us into drugs in the first place. When I first came to Riverside, I thought that I'd gotten into drugs just for the fun of it. But at Riverside I came to understand that drugs were an escape. I wasn't dealing with my parents' screwed up relationship and my mom's nasty habit of always dumping on me.

Neither of my parents is religious. But at Riverside, we prayed to God every day. We asked Him to give us the strength to overcome our weaknesses and the wisdom to know right from wrong. I felt good knowing there is a higher power in my life. I also learned that there is a purpose to my life. This is something that I was not taught at home.

I spent almost a year at Riverside. When I came home last spring, I felt that I wasn't ready to return to school. But now I'm at Seward Academy trying to make up as many credits as possible. Living at home is okay, mainly because my parents now pamper me a lot and try not to argue too much in front of me. Also, I have a wonderful girl friend who's twenty years old and a dancer. Next year, as soon as I become eighteen, we plan to get our own apartment. I will finally have a home of my own.

Delores Sanchez
16 years old

I grew up in a big apartment on the Grand Concourse in the Bronx. But as the years went by, the building began to deteriorate. The landlord never made repairs, and we'd go for weeks at a time with no hot water or heat. My mother tried to organize the tenants. She even took the landlord to court, and she urged the other tenants not to pay their rent. But she could never rally more than three other tenants, and eventually the landlord evicted us.

In the meantime, while we were still living in the Bronx, my little brother was born prematurely. He spent most of the first year of his life in and out of hospitals. We didn't know if he'd survive. The lack of hot water and heat made life very difficult for my mom and her new baby. Then, at the same time we were evicted from our building, my stepfather, and the only father I'd ever known and loved, died of a heart attack.

After we were forced out of our apartment in the Bronx, we tried to live with relatives. We stayed with our cousins for a while, but that didn't work out. Whenever anything was missing there'd be a big fight, and my mother was blamed. Then we went to my uncle's house. But he and I used to get into arguments all the time, and he decided that I couldn't live there any more.

At that point we went to the EAU, and we were assigned to a shelter in the Bronx. The shelter had a terrible reputation and was known as a haven for AIDS victims. My mother refused to accept the assignment. After my mother turned down a number of other assignments, we were finally sent to Jamaica Arms in Queens. We spent six months there. We had our own apartment and I went to a local junior high school in the neighborhood. Most of the other kids lived in private houses. I went to their homes, but I never invited them to mine. None of them knew my living situation.

What I remember most about that year, though, is all the time my mother spent with my brother in the hospital. He was forever throwing up, running high fevers, and being rushed to the emergency room. My mother never wanted to leave him alone in the hospital. So I didn't see much of my mother that year at the Jamaica Arms.

One of the social workers there helped us find our current apartment on the F.D.R. Drive. We were so happy to have our own place, but shortly after we moved in, my mother suffered a nervous breakdown. She was too depressed to do anything. It was so frightening to me. My mother was admitted to Mount Sinai Hospital. I was left alone with my brother who was three at the time. I was thirteen. I prayed for my mother's recovery, because I knew that if she didn't get well quickly, my brother and I would be placed in a home. Luckily, my mom was released a month later. I did miss a lot of school, and I've had a lot of making up to do.

I'm very happy to be living where I am. We never have problems with heat or hot water, and I don't miss the Bronx of my childhood at all.

Tito Reyes
17 years old

It was a Friday night. Me and my homeboy were driving around downtown. Just as we were passing Union Square, I saw some dude getting beaten up by six kids. I took my bat, ran out of the car, and busted one of the kid's heads. The next thing I knew some security guard was grabbing me. He called the cops, and I was taken to central booking.

Here I was trying to help some kid. And this is my reward—the Tombs. I was locked up with a bunch of crazy, stinking niggers. They fed me garbage, some smelly cheese not fit for human consumption. And then I got booked for assault.

I was found guilty and sent to Rikers. The whole scene was a real mess. My mother, a super straight lady who's never missed a day of church in her life, couldn't stop crying. My brother, who had just started college, acted as though I was a disgrace to the whole family. And my girlfriend, who'd just given birth to our son, needed me home working and helping her out.

I was in Rikers for five months. At first I was real scared, real depressed. I couldn't even eat. But then you get used to it. All I did was fight and deal drugs. You gotta fight just to get through a day there. If you act soft, you're finished. But you can't act too big either. You gotta just play it right.

Now I'm not into drugs, but just about everyone else there gets high. So I got into dealing cause I needed money. I needed money just to buy food there. You can't eat the slime they give you. And my girl needed money for our son. You know, pampers, clothes, trips to the clinic.

The way I got the drugs was kinda slick. My girl used to visit me every week. She'd carry with her these little balloons filled with cocaine. She hid them in her vagina. Right before she'd get to see me, she'd remove the balloons, wash them off, and put them into her mouth. Then she'd kiss me and I'd swallow them. You know the rest. It's all played out.

Most of the fights I got into was because of other niggers trying to take my drugs. I needed a Gilette just to survive. So my girl had our shoemaker from the Heights make a special hiding place in my black leather shoes. That's where she'd hide the Gilette. I used to go to church every Sunday at Rikers and I told the guards that my girl would be bringing me my dress shoes. So whenever she brought me my shoes, I renewed my supply of Gilettes.

Now doing drugs in Rikers is no big thing. Almost everyone gets high one way or another. Sometimes the dudes mix the stuff with toothpaste. Other times they empty their cigarettes of tobacco and fill them up with reefer or whatever they need to get high. The guards turn the other way. Sometimes they're even in on it. You can easily pay them off.

After I got outta Rikers, I continued dealing. I'd discovered an easy way to make money. I now attend George Washington High School, but most days I'm just hanging out selling drugs. Me and my girl and our kid—we need the money.

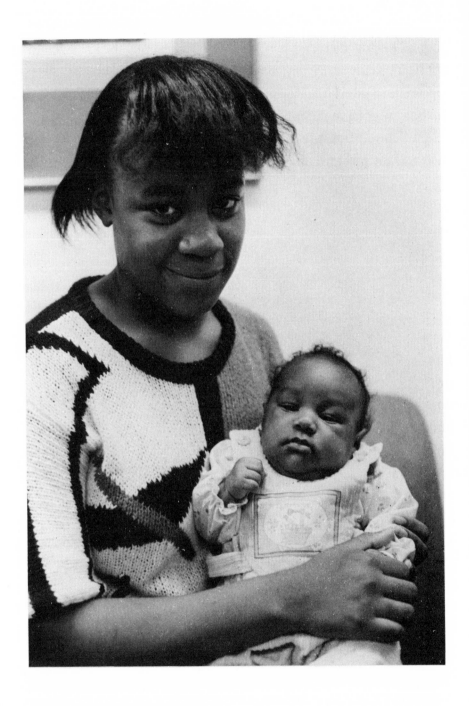

Diana Pineida
16 years old

I am my mom's only child. Sometimes she almost acted like she owned me. When I was eleven years old, she and my dad split up. He tried to stay in touch with me, but momma wouldn't let him. My mom is Puerto Rican, and my dad is Black. I know that my dad is somewhere down South now. I wish I could be in touch with him, but I don't know how to contact him. I don't know any of his relatives, and my mother refuses to tell me where he is. She doesn't even want his money.

My mother has always had a good job. She works for the telephone company and earns about $8.50 an hour. She used to spend almost all her salary on clothes for me. I was the best-dressed kid in the Mitchell Projects. In a way, I think my mother was trying to buy my love. I was a pretty devoted daughter until I started going to junior high school. Suddenly, my social life became real important to me. I stopped going to church with my mother, and started hanging out late with my friends. When I was fourteen, I became pregnant with Robbie.

That's when my mother threw me out of the house. She felt that I was a sinner. Also, I was an embarrassment to her. That, I think, was the main thing. I had embarrassed her. I never really considered getting an abortion. I didn't want to murder my own kid. I'm not religious like my mother, but I do believe that abortion is murder.

So I moved into my boyfriend's house. But soon after the baby was born, he and his family returned to Puerto Rico. I contacted my uncle, my mother's brother, and I think he might have taken my in. But my mother had gotten to him first and warned him, "If you take her it, you are finished with me." So here I was, fifteen years old, with a newborn baby and no where to go.

That's how I ended up at this shelter here on 157th Street. Just me and my son. Sometimes I feel as though he's the only friend I have. None of my friends from the Bronx know where I am. Robbie's only a year old, but I talk to him sometimes as if her were my companion. I tell him to hold on, not to give up.

The conditions here are terrible. Just the other day, one of the other mothers was raped in the shower. Last month, Robbie's father had sent him a bracelet for his first birthday, and one of the crackheads pushed little Robbie down the stairs and stole the bracelet from him. About half the guards are dealers, and they close their eyes when someone gets hurt.

I really want to return home. I've spoken to my uncle, and he tells me that my mother cries all the time. She really would like me to return home with Robbie, but she has too much pride. I'm hoping that if I just show up at my mother's door with Robbie, she won't turn us away. I'm planning to do that soon. I miss my mother so much, and I love her even though she's made this past year so difficult for me.

I also miss school a lot. I quit shortly before Robbie was born. But, according to my counselor at DeWitt Clinton, I have enough credits to go into the tenth grade. So as soon as I get my life back together, I plan to return to high school and get my diploma.

John Ruiz
17 years old

It started when I was thirteen years old. Instead of going to school, me and my best buddy spent the days rushing people. Whenever we spotted someone with gold, we held them up at knifepoint. We ripped off their gold, sold it and usually spent the money on reefer.

By the time I was fifteen I got into dealing cocaine. Both my older brothers were big time drug dealers, and I started to work for them. I made about $500 a day, but I only got to keep $150 of it. I turned over the rest of the money to my brothers.

If my mom suspected what was going on, she never let on. She probably figured she couldn't do anything about it anyway. She worked long hours at the post office and often stayed over at her boyfriend's house. My mother was hardly there when we were younger, and as the years went by she was home less and less. I never knew my father. I think he lives in Puerto Rico.

One night about two years ago, my older brother got high and started to load his gun. A shot accidentally went off and went right through our ceiling. My brother immediately broke out. About twenty minutes later the cops came and arrested me. They got me for possession of drugs and illegal possession of a gun. It seems our neighbors had called the cops. There was no way I could convince the cops that I wasn't the one who shot the gun.

Since this was my second offense—I had once been picked up for robbery—I was sent to Spofford for a year. There are about 500 kids in Spofford, mostly between the ages of thirteen to seventeen. Most of the kids there have been picked up for robbery and drug dealing. I couldn't believe how many kids I knew. It seemed as though half of the Avenue was there—practically my whole crew. There were four of us to a room, and since people knew me, nobody messed with me. I feel sorry for any kid who comes to Spofford who's soft. That kid's in big trouble. Everyone steals from a soft guy and beats on him.

We're treated like hard-core criminals by the security guards. There's lots of fighting going on, but we also get a chance to play pool and get high. It's not much different from summer camp. Smuggling drugs into Spofford is no problem. My homeboy used to bring me reefer hidden in his sock.

The most upsetting thing that happened to me at Spofford was finding out that one of my older brothers died. I read it in the papers.

Later, I got the whole story. It seems Angel was set up. My brother had been getting real big, and some big-time dealers from Brooklyn were afraid that he'd move into their turf. But they didn't let him know that. They set up a meeting with him in a parking lot in Brooklyn to discuss dividing up some turf. When Angel got there, they handcuffed him, stuffed cocaine into his mouth, and shot a bullet through his head. He died in an ambulance on the way to the hospital.

My mom didn't visit me even once the whole year I was at Spofford, and she never talked about my brother's death. I'm not sure it really bothered her that he was dead. She probably felt that only death could keep him out of trouble. But my other brother had a nervous breakdown after Angel was murdered.

I've been out of Spofford now for a few months, and I'm probably worse than I ever was. If I've changed at all, I've just gotten bolder. Just about every day me and my homeboy mug people at gun point. I almost never leave my house without a gun. We find our victims in subways, at the Seaport—especially when it's dark—and as they walk off the Brooklyn Bridge. We rush anyone who looks like he has some money or who's sporting some gold. Chinese people are the easiest.

We usually approach them, ask them the time, and then lure them to a place where we can rob them. We rarely have to knock them out. We go for rich white ladies, but they tend to scream so I usually have to punch them in the face to shut them up while my homeboy robs them. I only had to shoot someone once, and that's because we had some beef. Sometimes I have to slice people, but I can't really say I feel sorry. It's like my soul ain't working.

Much of the stealing me and my homeboy do is just for the thrill of it. We're really into motorcycles. Just last night we stole a motorcycle from Fifteenth Street and then lit it on fire at the

F.D.R. Drive. We also like to break into cars and sell the radios. I don't really worry about getting caught. I know just about half of Rikers anyway.

Yeah, I miss not having one real crib to live in. Maybe if my mother gave a damn I would have come back there after Spofford.

You see that van on the corner? That's my number one home right now.

Janice Rodriguez
16 years old

I never really got to know my father. I think he's spent time in every prison in the Northeast. He's a hoodlum. He's been in jail for selling drugs, stealing and assaulting cops. What I do remember about him are all his promises. All the promises that he broke. Every time he was out on parole, he came back home and promised my mother that he'd shape up. He never did. He always ended up splitting with everything me and my mother owned. The last time he came home was on a Sunday when I was eleven years old. He went to church with us, prayed for forgiveness, and then cut out on us that night with all my jewelry. I tell people that my father's dead. He might as well be.

But he probably isn't. The last time I saw him was two years ago when I was working in a clothing store on Fourteenth Street. Just as I looked up from the cash register, I saw my father buying an entire wardrobe for some cheap-looking woman. What made it even worse was that he made believe he didn't even know me. I haven't seen or heard from him since.

When I was twelve years old, my mother hooked up with my stepfather. Unlike my father, he had a solid job and didn't have a criminal record. My mother soon became pregnant, but my mother started having problems with my stepfather even before my brother was born. He was fine so long as he was sober. But when he was drunk, which was pretty often, he'd act real weird.

Shortly after my brother was born, I woke up early one morning to find my stepfather in bed with me. He was feeling me in the wrong places. I was horrified. I immediately ran to my mother. She went crazy. She scratched up his face and beat him with a hockey stick. He ran out of the house, naked, barefoot and bleeding. We thought we'd never see him again. My mother promised never to ever let him into the apartment again.

But about a month later, he reappeared and begged our forgiveness. He promised that he would never touch me again. My mother decided to give him one more chance. But I lived in terror of him, especially when he was drunk. I knew he'd been drinking that first time he tried to molest me.

At about the same time that my stepfather moved back in with us, I had a horrible experience at school. I was attending I.S. 383, a special intermediate school for the gifted in Brooklyn. A lot of the girls in my neighborhood resented me. They felt that I thought I was too smart for them. They were pressuring me to join their gang, but I refused. One day they followed me to school. As I was about to enter homeroom, all ten of them assaulted me. I remember screaming and praying real hard that some teacher would hear me and help me. But none of the teachers left their rooms. They were probably too frightened. I passed out and later woke up in the infirmary with a throbbing head and a bleeding eye. My mother picked me up and took me to the nearest emergency room. Three years later, I still get headaches and have to wear glasses. I also have nightmares all the time where I see myself getting beaten up by a gang of girls. My mother has filed a law suit against the school, and I'll probably collect some money when I'm seventeen.

About three months after my stepfather moved in with us, we had a party to celebrate my mother's thirtieth birthday. My stepfather got drunk and started dancing with me a little too close. I got real nervous and locked myself in the bedroom. My mother, who almost never drinks, was a little tipsy herself that night, and I was afraid that she wouldn't be able to help me if my stepfather tried anything. I was hoping to stay in my bedroom until the morning. But about midnight, my stepfather started banging on the door and demanded that I open it. When I refused to, he threatened to bang it down. I didn't know what to do. So I opened the door just a bit, and he pushed himself in. He said to me, "Tonight, you be ready for me."

I decided at that moment to kill myself. I had all these pills that the doctors gave me for the migraines I started getting after the attack. I combined about forty pills of Motrin, Co-Tylenol, and Darvocet. I fell asleep, woke up in a stupor and started vomiting. My mother took me to Bellevue Hospital. A young lady and an older man—both doctors—started asking me a lot of questions. I didn't want to tell them what had just gone down with my stepfather. Instead, I just told them that I was depressed and wanted to die. They transferred me to Kings County Hospital since we were living in Brooklyn at the time.

All I remember about my first day at Kings County is a big building full of crazy adults. I didn't know what to do. Hardly anybody talked to me. I spent the whole day by myself. The next day I was transferred to a ward for teenagers.

There were three other girls in my room. All of them had tried to kill themselves. There was Tanya, whose father had raped her and whose mother had abandoned her. She kept on drinking bottles of rubbing alcohol that she found in the hospital. I guess she figured she'd die that way. There was Delores, a gay girl, a real butch. When her mother found her in bed with a girlfriend, her mother threw her out. Delores then slashed her wrists and ended up here. I was real scared that Delores would hit on me. Just the idea sickened me. My closest friend was Wendy. She was Chinese, but acted like she was Black or Puerto Rican. Her parents couldn't understand her, and, I think, that's what made her crazy.

I was in the psychiatric ward at Kings County for three months. I hated it. I never felt safe. I think I was the only one there who wasn't put in a straight jacket. The girls were always getting into fights. The girls used their dinner knives and forks as weapons. We also had access to sharp tools in woodwork. The girls would fight over anything from potato chips to panties. The biggest fights took place Thursday nights. That was the one night we were allowed to use the telephone, and fights would always break out over whose turn it was.

Every day was the same at Kings County. We woke up at

7:30, cleaned our beds, got on line for a shower, went to their school—which was a joke because it was so easy—and then had group. Group was when we were supposed to talk about our problems. But I never told anyone about what had gone down with my stepfather or what life had been like with my real father. I don't think too many of the girls were honest in group. I also don't think any of the nurses, doctors, or social workers really cared about us. After group a lot of the girls would go to the bathroom to get high. Drugs—mostly marijuana—was brought in by visitors. The girls would smoke it in the bathroom and then spray perfume to hide the odor.

The only day I looked forward to was Sunday. That was when we went to church and got to see the boys. The rest of the week they were kept away from us. The problem was that the two cutest boys were two brothers who had killed their parents. There was another guy, Tony, who I felt real sorry for. His body was all lopsided. It seems he was running away from his alcoholic mother who had been beating him and he got hit by an ice-cream truck. He was always crying.

One of the most frightening things that happened was when Leticia, a girl who had killed her father, started running around with a butcher knife. I thought she was going to kill me. Then one night my gay roommate started kissing me. I told one of the social workers how scared I was, and she asked me if I wanted to go home. But I was afraid to go home. My mother kept on promising me that she had gotten rid of my stepfather, but I didn't trust her. I didn't trust him either. I was afraid that he'd find me. I told the social workers that I wanted to go into a group home. Finally, my mother convinced me to go home.

I've been home for over a year now, but things aren't good. My mother has a new boyfriend. I hate him. We ignore each other, but I don't like the way he treats my mother. He always speaks down to her. I also worry about my little brother. He's real hyper and nervous. I'm depressed all the time. I'm thinking of moving in with a cousin who's living in my grandmother's apartment on the Lower East Side. My grandma's away in Puerto Rico. But my mother wants me at home. She uses me to babysit all the time, and makes me feel guilty when I don't want to. I'm sorry her life is so messed up, but I got to worry about my own. I really don't know what to do.

Eric Johnson
15 years old

I grew up in the Park Slope section of Brooklyn. Everything was cool until five years ago. That's when my brother was arrested for rape. He was innocent. He never raped anyone. It was a set up. He had been having trouble with some of the white boys in the neighborhood. A white lady was paid off to say that my brother raped her. The cops forced him to confess to something he didn't do. He was seventeen at the time. He was sent to a juvenile detention center upstate and then the following year he was put in prison. He's never gotten into any fights with anyone, but he was denied parole after three years. He's supposed to be coming out this June. At first he was all my mother talked about. Now she tries not to even think about him.

After the trouble with my brother, we left Park Slope. My mother and I moved into my aunt's apartment in Coney Island. I liked it there. I was in P.S. 145 and went to school every day. I was a pretty good student. But then one day I came home from school to find out that we had been evicted. It seems that my aunt hadn't been paying her rent. My mom was working at a video store and she would have helped my aunt out. But my mom didn't know that my aunt hadn't been paying her rent. By the time my mom found out, it was too late to do anything about it.

After we were evicted, we spent six months in Forbell, a shelter on the border between Brooklyn and Queens. I remember our first night there. My mom and I were real nervous. Forbell consists of three levels with about one hundred beds on each level. What bothered me the most about Forbell was the lack of privacy. Also, I had no independence. It was like being in jail. I couldn't leave without my mom's permission. My mom was working in the video store at the time so, except for the hours I spent in school, I was stuck in the shelter with nothing to do. And the food was terrible. Everything they served us tasted funny.

Then we were transferred to Traveler's. Traveler's is a hotel in Queens. We were so happy to have our own room there. We even had our own hot plate so my mom was able to prepare her own food. But there were problems at Traveler's. The ladies there were always getting into fights. They fought over everything. Also, we weren't allowed to have any guests over. So the ladies used to sneak in their boyfriends, and the only friends I had were the other hotel kids. That's when I got into playing hooky. The kids never wanted to go to school. Instead, we hung out and drank beer.

We lived in Traveler's for two years. Then we had to leave. My mother's welfare payments had stopped, and we couldn't afford to live in a hotel. I'm not sure why she wasn't eligible for welfare anymore. Then my mom and I had to split up. She went to live with her sister in Brooklyn, and I went to live with my grandmother in Staten Island. I lived with my grandmother for one year.

Now my mom and I are back together at the shelter on Catherine Street. There's a new policy at Catherine Street with two families sharing one room. So me and my mother are together with another lady and her fourteen year old son. What I don't like about Catherine is all the drugs. About 75 percent of the people are doing one drug or another. The most popular drug here is crack which is sold in $10 vials. Drugs are sold outside the shelter—mainly by teenage boys—but there are also people inside selling them. I also don't like when the guards mess with the ladies. I feel that they are taking advantage of them.

We hope to be out of Catherine by the end of this month. My mom is waiting for an apartment anywhere. But all I want is my own place in Brooklyn. I don't want to have to live with anyone, including my own mother.

Tammy Roberts
15 years old

Things were okay until my mom started using crack. I used to go to school every day, and we used to go to church on Sundays. But once mama started doing crack, everything changed. For one, she got so behind in paying rent that we were evicted from our apartment in Bushwick. That's how I ended up here at the shelter on Catherine Street. And to help my mother out, I got into shoplifting. And then everything else followed.

My mom needed money just to have enough crack to make it through the day. And I felt that I owed it to her to help her out. I'm her only child, and we were always close. So I started stealing things. I stole anything that I thought I could sell: Walkmen, clothes, appliances, jewelry. I became real tight with one of the other girls at the shelter who'd been shoplifting most of her life. She was real slick. She knew where to get the goods and how to get rid of them real fast. We worked together. We mostly did department stores. We never got caught.

One day when I was hungry—the food at the shelter is terrible—I decided to shoplift some cans of tuna fish from the Pathmark here on Madison Street. I was by myself, and I got caught. I was taken to a back room, and I suddenly had an idea. I decided to rub up real close to the security guard who was arresting me. I gave him what he wanted. Not only did he drop all charges against me, but he gave me a brand new fifty dollar bill.

I had discovered a new way to make money. I didn't need to shoplift anymore, and I could do this without my friend. Whenever I saw some lonely guy who looked kinda shy and kinda rich, I'd rub up to him. I know guys think I'm cute, and this worked out well for me. I'd tell the sucker that I needed money, and I'd ask him to help me out. Usually he'd take me to his car, and I'd make him feel real good real fast. He often slipped me a fifty. Some guy once gave me a hundred dollar bill. Most of the guys were real generous. So even though I hated what I was doing, I liked the money. And I knew that my mother needed it real bad.

Meanwhile, my mom started mixing the crack with heroin, and was real messed up. I started feeling terribly depressed. I couldn't believe that I'd actually been selling my body. I felt so cheap. About two months ago, I started getting high myself. One of the kids here at the shelter who supplies my mom started selling me crack, too. I just wanted to forget all of the problems my mama and I were having.

About a month ago, I started feeling strange. My glands were swollen. My insides felt like they were torn apart. The doctor tested me for AIDS, and the results came back positive. I guess that means I'm gonna die. But it don't really make no difference to me now. I don't look so good anymore, but I still sell my body to anyone who wants it. I say to myself, "What the hell! It's all part of life. Ain't it?"

Arcadio Santiago
15 years old

It started last year. On my way home from J.H.S. 56 I spotted a pair of sneakers that I really wanted. But I just couldn't afford them. There was no way. So, as I was riding my bike down Pitt Street, I decided to grab this lady's purse. It had over $100 in cash. I had discovered a quick, easy way to make money.

For the next two months I did most of my purse snatching from the seat of my bike. Pitt Street was my main turf. But then I got bolder and greedier. My homeboy and I started holding up people at knife point. Carlos would hold our victim in a head-lock and I would grab the money. Our victims were almost always Chinese women in their twenties. They always seemed to have cash on them, and they never put up a fight. We worked the seaport, the area around Broadway-Lafayette, and the block behind the church here on Grand Street. We'd also wait outside the Essex Theater and follow anyone who looked like an easy mark.

I never felt right about what I was doing. I said to myself, "These people probably need the money as much as I do." Once I actually threw back a purse to a lady I had just mugged at the seaport. She was begging me to return it to her, and I figured she might have had some important papers in there, like her birth certificate or her social security card. I always felt scared when I was holding people up, and, afterwards, I felt guilty. Also, I didn't really need the money. I don't do any drugs, so I'd spend the money on sneakers and jackets or any gear that would make me feel good. But I couldn't stop. Mugging became a habit. I just made sure that I didn't hurt anybody.

Then one evening my luck ran out. Me and my homeboy were robbing a Chinese lady at the East Broadway F Train station. She screamed real loud and the cops heard her. My homeboy hopped on the next train to Brooklyn, but I tried to run out of the station. I was instantly caught with the $82 I had just stolen.

I was taken to the 7th Precinct Station on Pitt Street. The cops called my mother. She was real angry. We were given a date to appear in Family Court. Since I was only fourteen at the time, I was considered a Y.D. (young delinquent). We appeared in court about two weeks later, but the woman whom I robbed never showed up. This went on about five times. My mom would accompany me to court and we'd wait for the Chinese lady to testify against me. But she never showed up. Eventually my case was thrown out of court.

Two months later my homeboy and I decided to rob a taxi cab driver. We figured it would be an easy job and good money. We grabbed a cab on 47th on Broadway at about 6:30 in the evening. My friend had a black jack, and I held a knife to the guy's neck. The guy—a white boy—was stunned and didn't mutter a word. But somebody else must have seen us because a cop suddenly appeared. My homeboy somehow managed to cut out, but I got stuck inside the cab. I was taken to a precinct uptown. The cops called my mom and I was sent to Spofford for eight days. I kept to myself the whole time. I didn't hang out. I didn't want to be part of the scene there. I don't really think of myself as a criminal.

About a month after I was released from Spofford, I got into trouble again. This time it wasn't my fault. I was hanging out on the Avenue with my friends. A police van arrived and a whole bunch of kids started hurling bricks at the cops. The kids ran as the cops came out of the van. I didn't run, and so I was the only one the cops caught. They didn't believe I was innocent. I was accused of assaulting a policeman. I was sent to a special school known as ATD (Alternative to Detention) or Probation School. I stayed there for two months, and I returned home every night to sleep.

I've just been released and I've promised myself to stay out of trouble. My mother is threatening to send me to a group home if I mess up again. But I owe it to my mom not to mess up. I had an older brother who died when he was eighteen. He'd be twenty-four years old today if he were still alive. He drowned in a fishing accident. He was probably high at the time. It really broke my mother up, and I don't want to give her any more pain. Also, I need to set a good example for my twelve-year-old brother.

Right now I'm looking for a job, any job that can keep me out of trouble.

Panama Watkins
15 years old

I know that the Prince George Hotel has a terrible reputation, but to me it is home. I have lived here for two years, and it's the best home I ever had.

I grew up in a dreary apartment in Crown Heights. I never felt safe there. Just walking through the streets to get home from the closest subway station was like walking through a war zone. About three years ago, the landlord died. The building was sold, and my mother couldn't afford the new rent. So we moved in with my grandmother. But things didn't work out. My grandmother has high blood pressure, and it was too much for her to have my mother, my sister and me living with her. After six months of staying with my grandmother, my mother went to the EAU and we were assigned to a shelter on Catherine Street.

I didn't like the shelter. It was too crowded, and I didn't have any privacy. Here in the Prince George we have our own room. What I like most about living in the Prince George Hotel is its location. I am right near mid-town. There is always something to do. In Crown Heights, there was never anything happening, just muggings and shoot-outs. I don't miss anything about my old neighborhood.

The only problem I have here is dealing with my mother's constant worrying. About 95 percent of the teenagers here deal drugs. Just about every one I know sells $5 vials of crack. And my mother is afraid that me and my sister will start using drugs. But she really doesn't have to worry. I'm not interested in that life, and neither is my sister. The other thing my mother worries about is my getting pregnant. About half the teenagers who are here have babies with them. They are living here because their mothers threw them out of their houses. But I'm not about to bring home any babies. I'm a baby myself.

School is the only problem I've had since we lost our apartment in Brooklyn. I used to go to school every day. But last year, I cut a lot. Most of the teenagers here don't go to school. They just hang out instead. My cousin influences me not to go to school, and now missing school is my worst habit.

There is talk now of closing down this hotel. My mother wants to move back to Brooklyn, and our social worker is helping us find an apartment in some projects near our old neighborhood. But I don't ever want to leave Manhattan. I like it here. It is the place I call home.

Edwin Santana
14 years old

I always loved cars. From the time I was real little. When I was ten years old, this guy Sal taught me how to drive. He was an auto mechanic, and I used to go by his garage on Houston Street almost every day. After a few lessons, I sat in the driver's seat and Sal used to sit next to me. I'd go cruising all over town. It felt great.

The next year, I started breaking into cars. Practically every car that I liked, I managed to get into. Usually I had to break its windows. Sometimes I'd just drive someplace and sleep in it. Other times I'd strip it. I'd usually be able to sell its radio or tape deck for about $25.

By the time I was twelve I almost never went to school. Instead, me and my homeboys would steal cars. We stole at least a car a day. We used to take the train up to fancy white neighborhoods and break into any car that looked good. We then sold the car. We'd sell it for like $1500 and then split the money between us. We then spent the money on chill clothes. And we'd go dancing. Life was good. I was caught a few times, but I was always released immediately.

The only problem I was having was with my mother. She knew what I was into, and she tried to stop me. She bought this big lock for the inside of the apartment. She thought she was gonna keep me locked in. So we used to be getting into these fights almost every day. But, somehow, I always managed to get the key. My mom kept on blaming my friends. But the truth is that I was the one to blame. Nobody else got me into stealing cars. It was my own doing. Lotsa times I worked by myself.

After I was into this for about a year and a half, I got seriously caught. What happened was that I was driving a stolen car down the F.D.R. I noticed a police car following me, and I panicked. I ran over three cops. One of them got seriously hurt. It was in the news and all. All my friends saw me on the tube. I wish I coulda seen it. I wonder if they told a bunch of lies about me or what.

I was taken in handcuffs to the 90th precinct. About a dozen cops—all white—beat the crap out of me. I was in so much pain that I couldn't even cry. I wish I could have gotten their badge numbers and reported them. But I didn't think about it at the time. I couldn't think of nothing, accept maybe staying alive. After they beat me up, they handcuffed me to a chair and left me there all day. They called my mother. About an hour later, she arrived at the precinct crying. She rushed over to me and beat me some more. Just what I needed, huh?

My father stayed outside. He has diabetes and my mother was afraid that if he saw me, he'd get seriously sick.

The following afternoon, I was taken to Lincoln Hospital cause my eyes were black and blue and my face was all puffed up. From there I was put in a wagon with metal bars and taken to Spofford. When I got there, they gave me this dumb blue outfit that didn't fit me, and these lame Converse sneakers that hurt my feet.

Spofford's okay, though. I knew a lot of the kids there, including some from the Lower East Side. Every day at Spofford's the same. They'd wake us up every morning at six o'clock by pounding on our doors. If we didn't immediately get up, they'd come in and roll us out of our covers and onto the floor. Then if we wanted to, we could take showers. I always took my showers in the morning, 'cause that's when the showers were the emptiest. There was only two guys to a shower. But practically every morning, another fight broke out in the shower room. Usually it was over a piece of soap. But it could be over anything. 'Cause that's how the guys at Spofford are. They fight over anything. Lotsa stuff that's not worth fighting about. But you can't back down, if you know what I mean.

After I took my shower, I had to make my bed and clean up my room. By the time I got back to my room, whatever I had from the previous day was usually stolen. Candy bars, gum—everything I earned by being on the highest level. Even my Walkman. Everything my mother ever brought for me was stolen from me. I only stole once and that was because my pants didn't fit me and I had to find ones that did.

Then they gave us breakfast. Not worth talking about. The steak they give you there tastes like rubber. After breakfast we went to school. That was the best part of the day, 'cause it was the only time of day that we got to be with the girls. There were about twelve kids in a class with at least three girls in each class. The teachers were okay, too. There was this real nice bald-headed guy who really cared about us. But fights used to break out in class a lot, over dumb things like pencils, paper and other stupid stuff. So I never got to learn very much. I never really learned anything in regular school either, after the first grade, anyway. Reading is the worst; I hate it.

After school we used to watch MTV 'til about 4 o'clock. And then we'd either go swimming, work out at the gym or play video games. No quarters needed; matter of fact there wasn't no money allowed in the whole place. No matter where we were, fights would break out. We weren't supposed to have weapons, but they were smuggled into us by visitors all the time. Like your homeboy would throw a Gilette or shank into a tree and then you'd go get it. It wasn't hard to get drugs either. Visitors used to bring them in their socks or underwear and then pass them to us when no one was looking. Most of the time the guards ignored it, but once there was a big bust when fifty vials of crack was found in one of the rooms. I'm glad it wasn't mine. All I ever did was some reefer anyway. Drugs aren't my thing. Cars are.

My mom used to visit me about three times a week, and I kept on thinking that at any day I'd be out of Spofford and on my way home. But after four months at Spofford, I was told that I had to go to the Tryon School, a juvenile detention center upstate, for eighteen months. I couldn't believe it. But there was nothing I could do about it. So I decided to be real good and hope that I'd be let out sooner. The worst part of being upstate was being so far away from my family and friends.

Even though we were living in cottages it felt like a real lock-up. I was so lonely there. I hated it. Round trip fare from New York City was $55 so my mom could only come about twice a month. I did meet a girl, though, who I really liked and that's what got me through each day. She'll be coming out next week, and I can't wait to see her. She's white and Italian, I think. She got a boyfriend but she said she don't care. Hey, I got a girl-friend too. What she don't know won't hurt her. Also, one of the social workers there, this black guy, was real cool and taught me how to play the steel drums. I really dug it. I have some good tapes of playing some songs like John Lennon's "Imagine." Never thought I'd even listen to that stuff. This guy and his wife even invited me to his house when he got out. He got in trouble when he was my age too.

Because I was real good, they let me out after four months. All the way back I had this big smile on my face. I've been home now for about six weeks. I'm so happy to be free and do anything I want. I learned my lesson and I stay far away from cars now. They don't even tempt me any more, even though my friends still do it. It's all behind me now.

The only problem now is school. I'm in Special Ed., and I hate it. The teachers are okay, but it's me. I never liked school. When my guidance counselor told me that I don't have enough credits to graduate junior high school, I started cutting out. I really don't expect to be spending much more time in school. At least half of the kids in my neighborhood have already dropped out. I'd like to get a job. Really, I'll do anything with cars. Otherwise, I would like to be on the staff of a place like Tryon and help kids in trouble.

Shanita Dixon
17 years old

Things were never really cool with my mother. She didn't take drugs or drink or anything like that, but she had her highs and lows. She was completely unpredictable. When she got into her bad moods, she would leave it out on me. If she was feeling lousy for whatever reason, I was the one who suffered. When I was younger, she used to beat me all the time with a wet ironing cord. Sometimes she just used the iron. I still have scars all over my legs.

When I was fourteen years old, I became pregnant with Mikie. My boyfriend Richie offered to help me out at the time. After Mikie was born, Richie moved in with me and my mom and took care of Mikie while I worked. I worked as a cashier at Gristedes and made just about enough money to cover my expenses. Shortly after Mikie was born, I became pregnant again. Richie did not want me to have the baby. I didn't want to abort it. Richie and I started arguing a lot, and eventually I found out that he had another girlfriend who was also pregnant. Richie moved out.

After my second son, David, was born, I saw Richie only occasionally. Things were not good between us. Almost every time we were together, we fought. Sometimes, though, he babysat while I went to work. One day I came home from work to find Richie, Mikie and David gone. At first I thought they'd just stepped out for awhile. But soon it was midnight, and they hadn't returned. I panicked. I called Richie's mother. It seems that Richie had run off with the kids to some relatives in Baltimore. His mother wouldn't tell me much more. I contacted the police and within two weeks, the kids were found in Richie's aunt's house in Baltimore. I went down to Baltimore to get my kids back, and that's when I met Robert.

We were both sixteen at the time. Robert was cute and kind. We fell in love, and Robert offered to come back with me to New York to help me out with the boys. I guess he kinda felt sorry for me. My mother, at first, liked Robert a lot. She was glad to have him living with us. When he first came up to New York, he got a job doing construction work and helped us all out. He paid for just about all our food. But the construction company folded, and Robert was out of work. He had a few odd jobs here and there, but the money wasn't good. Robert was real honest, and he never tried to make easy money. Robert started feeling depressed and hung around the house a lot.

At about the same time, my mother hooked up with another woman. She'd had a number of gay relationships through the years, but this time she was in love. She invited her new lover to live with her and threw me, Robert, and my two kids out of the house.

That's when I started living in a shelter. Me and the two kids were placed in a shelter downtown. I had to sneak Robert in all the time. It was real hard on all of us. There were shoot-outs in the halls and drug dealers roaming around as though they owned the place. Everything we had was stolen from us. The halls stank from piss and worse. This was no place to raise children. But it was the children that kept me alive. People felt protective towards me because they knew that I had two young kids to take care of. Also, they looked out for my kids. Mikie is kinda hyper, but David is slow. He is fourteen months, but he doesn't walk yet. He is just now wearing the clothes that Mikie wore when Mikie was five months old. David was born prematurely when I was in my seventh month, and the doctor keeps telling me that he will catch up. Sometimes I worry about him.

Anyway, living in a shelter put a strain on my relationship with Robert. He felt terrible that he couldn't support me and that we couldn't afford our own apartment. About two months ago, Robert started acting real depressed.

We went for a walk in Central Park, and Robert started playing with a rope. I thought he was just playing, but before I knew what was happening, he was dead. He died in my arms.

I just wanted to die, too. I called up my mother whom I hadn't spoken to in a while. I told her what had happened. I told her that I wanted to kill myself. Her only response was, "If you kill yourself, you better take your kids with you, 'cause I'm sure as hell not gonna take care of them."

After Robert died, I felt as thought I couldn't go on. I still break down every time I talk about him. Sometimes I talk to him as if he was still alive. About three weeks ago, me and the kids moved into my older brother's studio apartment. It's real small and hard on my brother, but he's glad that he can help me out.

I dropped out of school right before Mikie was born. But if I can get some day care for the kids, I'd like to go back.

Joshua Winkler
14 years old

My parents were fighting for years. They finally got divorced when my mother was pregnant with my little brother Joey. I remember my father a little. He was the quieter one. My mother didn't let the divorce go through for years. She was always fighting him, and he wanted to be left alone.

He finally left us alone and started a whole new family. I don't see his new kids, and I don't see my real twin sisters and older brother either. For the last few years nobody has seen my mother or Joey. The police think my mother has got him somewhere, but they just can't track her down. My mother is harder to find than "America's Most Wanted."

She changed her name many times in the years that she lived with Joey and me. We changed houses a lot, and went to live in Florida a few times. Even scarier, she changed her face too. The policemen I spoke to when they were looking for Joey couldn't figure out how she had the money for plastic surgery. I never saw her at any jobs making money.

Before me and Joey were brought to group homes my mother made things pretty bad for us. I didn't eat enough and I always had torn sneakers with the toes sticking out. My mother would mostly hit me and scream at both of us. I have partial vision in my right eye because of a detached retina. My doctors said that my mother didn't knock my eye out, but she was responsible for not getting me to a hospital for many years.

She never let us out when she could help it. She was afraid of everybody. When my grandma called, my mother's mother, every word that we said on the pay phone had to be approved by my mother first. Grandma was the only one who knew where we lived and even she could never call us. Everything had to be a big secret, like there were spies listening on the phone and waiting in the hallways. My counselors tell me that my mother isn't evil. She's just mentally ill.

When I was thirteen I took Joey and ran to a policeman. Ever since that time I have been in group homes and with foster families. I like group homes better. I don't know what to do in a family. Families are only something on TV.

I don't do so good in regular school and I am now in a religious Jewish school where things are better. I am getting to know about who I am and what I am supposed to do. The religious school was my father's idea, because he got more religious since he got away from my mother. My father visits and sends money, but I don't see his new family.

Me and my brother were first together in group homes.

Then we were separated in different foster homes, and for about a year now he has been missing.

Everybody thinks my mother got him back. The social workers and police ask me if I've seen him or my mother, but I haven't. They should believe me, because I never want to see her again.

Maria Colon
15 years old

My mom is 56 years old and not in good health. She's always suffered from asthma, and now she has high blood pressure. The doctor's always telling her to relax, but she can't. I feel sorry for her. She can't really deal with me. The only other person who lives with us is my brother. He's thirty-two and keeps to himself. My father lives only a few blocks away, but he never visits us. I only go to him when I need money.

The problems started about three years ago, when I was thirteen years old. I started hanging out all night. The earliest I'd come home was four in the morning. I'd stay out all night with my friends, smoking herb, drinking beer, and just chillin'. My mom kept on warning me that if this kept up she was going to put me in a home. I guess I didn't really believe her. One morning when I came home at seven o'clock in the morning, my mom accused me of stealing one hundred dollars from her drawer. She told me that she just couldn't take it anymore and was going to put me in a home. She didn't want no daughter of hers coming home pregnant or dead.

I was horrified. I didn't know what to do. So I decided to run away. I ran to my boyfriend's house. He only lives three blocks away. His mom knew that my mother had petitioned the courts and had gotten a warrant for my arrest, so she let me stay there with them. But I couldn't leave the apartment. I was afraid to be seen. My mom must have tracked me down because Monday morning, after I'd been staying in Pedro's house for a whole week, two policemen rang the doorbell. I hid. Pedro's sister invited the cops in and told them that I was afraid to go home. In the meantime, I managed to escape. After a two-hour chase, the police finally caught me and brought me to court.

I begged the court to let me go to my cousin's house, but I guess my cousin didn't want me there. I was taken instead to a foster home in Harlem. It was terrible. I'd never been to Harlem, and I wasn't used to being around Black people. And here I was with a Black woman and her seven children. I couldn't tell which were her real children and which kids were staying with her. I couldn't stop crying. I called my mother and begged her to take me home. I promised her I'd never cause her any more problems. She said she'd speak to me the following day.

The next day a social worker came to pick me up. She said she was taking me to a home on East 17th Street. I was so embarrassed. I hadn't had a chance to take a shower and my hair was a real mess. But the social worker was real nice, and I began to feel a little less scared and a little more comfortable. She took me to Euphrasia, a diagnostic center for teenagers with problems. As soon as I got there, I started crying. I couldn't stop crying. I stayed there for two months. I cried every morning, every night and I broke down just about every time I spoke to a social worker.

I couldn't believe that my mom had actually thrown me out. I called her my second night at Euphrasia and again begged her to take me home. It was the day before my birthday. How could she do this to me on my birthday? The next day, she visited me with a cake and roses but with no plans to take me home.

Two months later, my mother agreed to allow me to return home. I promised to maintain a nine o'clock curfew at all times. I told her I'd start coming to school. I even promised to get a job. Also, I had to promise to continue seeing a social worker on a regular basis.

I've been home now for the past four months. I'll never again take my mother for granted. I never break my curfew. I'm afraid to. I know that my mom would immediately put me back in a home. I even have a job now. I work as a cashier in a Pioneer supermarket. But school's another story. I just can't get used to staying in school, and I usually end up cutting out with my two best friends after official class. I haven't told my social worker that I've been messing up in school, but I guess that at some point soon I'm gonna have to deal with that. I just don't want to think about it now.

What I'd really like to do is get out of the Lower East Side. I'd like to leave New York and buy a home in Florida. That is my dream. But for the next three years I plan to live with my mother. Until I am on my own, I don't want to be without a home again.

Ricky Calderon
18 years old

The first time was for assault with a deadly weapon. I was cold dissed by a teacher. I had to make the bitch pay for making me look like a faggot in front of everyone. The second time was also for assault, but I was innocent. This friend of mine, or I should say ex-friend, was breaking into my apartment when he thought I was out. I told him I was going to be out, and that's why the little bastard knew to come rob me then. But I was home. He got in through my fire escape. I cut him up pretty good. I was defending myself and my property. Now how are you going to call that "assault?" They only were out to get me because of the first time.

I was already eighteen so they put me in Sing Sing. This time it was for twenty-six months. They should have put me into Rikers where I would be with my uncle. He's only four years older than me, but he would have protected me. I could have been with more of my people. My uncle is very loyal to our people.

He only sold drugs to blacks and whites, but he'd never sell to Spanish people.

That's what you need in these places, your own people. The fighting is mostly a battle between big groups. It's a war between those you know and those that you don't want to know. Everybody has a knife or something, so you have to make one with your own hands.

We were woken up at around 6:30 every morning for no reason. Just to hassle us. We were counted every morning and two more times after that. We were led to the dining rooms for breakfast. But who feels like eating their slop so early in the morning? The food is no good. You gotta get food from the outside if you want something decent. The drugs also came in from the visitors. Anybody who was soul kissing was getting a balloon passed to them.

After breakfast, we all go to our jobs. Mostly it lets the wrong guys get a hold of the wrong tools. Job time and recreation time can be the most dangerous, because it's easier for the guards to turn around and tune out when something happens. If you're not with some of your people, then you better be one big, tough dude.

It's all in the deal of the cards. You don't know who is going to be in your cell. If he's okay he'll pound the meat and if not you don't know what he'll do. I'm not one of those faggots sleeping with his butt up in the air, but you got to do some things to stay alive. I tried to get myself in solitary confinement as much as possible. It was the safest place. I never had to worry about getting raped. Guys were getting raped here all the time. There are many more faggots here than at Rikers. If you drop your soap in the shower here, you better not pick it up.

I just don't wanna think about it no more. The place is hazardous to your health.

Carlotta Acosta
18 years old

I remember when my mom married my stepfather. I was eight years old. I was so happy to have a father. I never really knew mine. I think he lives in California. I know my mother hates him.

I was real close to my stepfather, and I trusted him. When he first started to molest me, I couldn't believe it. I couldn't believe that he would betray me like that. My mother is a nurse at Bellevue and she works the night shift three times a week. When I was about fourteen years old, my father made his first appearance in my bedroom when my mom wasn't home one night. I was horrified. I thought I was having a nightmare. When I told my mother what had happened, she didn't believe me. She accused me of making up stories to get attention. She was real depressed that she couldn't get pregnant by my stepfather, and she desperately wanted his baby. That's all she thought about.

I was afraid to stay home at night when my mother was working. So I got in with a crowd that hung out all night. My boyfriend was dealing drugs, and occasionally I snorted coke. If I stayed in at night when my mom wasn't home, my stepfather would make his way into my room and try to have sex with me. I tried to be home as little as possible.

Whenever I told my mom what my stepfather was doing to me, she accused me of lying. I ran away from home and moved into my boyfriend's house. About a week later, I was arrested for dealing and sent to the Lakeside Detention Home upstate. My mother had sent the police to get me.

I spent a year and a half at Lakeside. It was terrible and not much better than being at home with my stepfather. The only time I felt safe at Lakeside was when I was in school. When we weren't in school, the girls were always getting into fights. Once I had to slice up somebody's face. The bitch tried to take my sneakers. I was put into solitary for two days. You always had to be tough at Lakeside. Weapons were smuggled in, and there were guns and knives everywhere.

Just about everybody got high. Our visitors smuggled in all kinds of drugs, usually in their socks. The guards even sold it. Nobody cared. Lots of fights broke out over drugs. My roommate, who was in for armed robbery, got stabbed real bad.

After I left Lakeside, I tried living at home again. Things were worse than ever. My mother had started getting high on coke and was talking real crazy. She was real depressed that she couldn't have a baby. She asked me to get inseminated with my stepfather's sperm and give the baby to her. She had to be joking.

After I was back home for about a month, my stepfather raped me again. This time I got pregnant. I know that my son who is now three months old is my stepfather's child. When I told my mother I was pregnant, she told me that she wanted my baby. She denied, though, that it was her husband's child. She kept on insisting that it was my boyfriend who got me pregnant. But I had broken up with my boyfriend, and Jose couldn't possibly be anyone else's kid but my stepfather's.

I didn't want my mother to take my baby away from me and I didn't want my stepfather to ever touch me again. So I had to run away. Luckily, I met Hector who treats me real good and treats Jose like his own son. Hector has his own apartment and makes a lot of money dealing drugs. People come in from all over to buy the stuff here. Hector makes about $300 a day and gets to keep most of it. I haven't seen my mother since my baby was born, but Hector tells me that she buys her coke from him. Some of Hector's customers pay for their drugs with food stamps, and I use the food stamps to buy food for me, Hector and Jose. I am so glad to be away from my stepfather and my mother. I hope I never have to see them again. I just found out today that I'm pregnant again. I know that the baby is Hector's. If my mother knew, I know that she would try to take my baby away again.

Steve Davis
16 years old

My childhood was hell. When I was a year old, my mother married my stepfather. He never liked me. In fact, he hated me. My earliest memory is of him locking me in my room for four days. My mother had gone to the hospital to give birth to my little brother. I was three years old at the time. My father let me out only to eat.

As I grew older, my stepfather treated me worse than a slave. He smacked me, tripped me and threw things at me for no reason. After he'd trip me, he'd curse at me and call me clumsy, then trip me again. Also, he had me doing all the housework.

My mother works in a daycare center, and my father has a night job as a door man. During the day when my mother wasn't home, my father expected me to keep the house clean. It became my job to dust the furniture, sweep the floors, wash the dishes, and take out the garbage. After I'd finish, he'd purposely mess up the house again to give me more work to do. My stepfather often kept me home from school to keep the house in order.

When he wasn't sleeping or eating he was getting high. When my mother came home from work, she often ended up beating my stepfather. She was always angriest on my stepfather's pay days, because he never came home with the money he'd been making. He usually spent it on cocaine before he reached our apartment. She'd either hit him with her hands or throw things at him. During the day he evened the score by beating me up.

As I grew older, things only got worse. He constantly criticized me. He'd tell me that he didn't like the way I dressed and he'd rip up my clothes. He criticized my voice and complained that I sounded and acted like a girl. For no reason at all he'd beat me with a belt. I still have a large welt on my leg from one of my stepfather's beatings. I guess I'll always have it.

When I was about eight years old, my mother's brother began spending weekends with us. He was about twenty-five-years old and had just split up with his wife. One Saturday morning I woke up next to him to find him doing strange things to me. I didn't know what to do. I was afraid to tell my parents. My stepfather would have killed the both of us, and my mother wouldn't have believed me. My uncle continued to sexually abuse me until I was about twelve years old. He never knew when to stop. At the beginning I was horrified, but then I got used to it. I always hated it. I felt used.

I did complain to my mother, though, about the way my stepfather was treating me. I explained to her how I was afraid to be in the house alone with him. I described to her how he treated me. How impossible it was for me when she wasn't home during the day. My mother didn't believe me. She kept on telling me that it was my imagination. Finally, I decided that I couldn't take it any more. I made up my mind to kill myself. On my thirteenth birthday, I drank a pint of peroxide and swallowed a bottle of aspirins. I didn't succeed in killing myself, and I got both my parents even angrier at me. My mother was furious. She did not want the hospital to know that I had attempted suicide. She was afraid that I would be taken away from her. So she made up this story to the doctor that she had poured a pint of peroxide into a glass to clean her scraped knee and that I accidentally drank it. The doctor didn't believe her.

After I was released from the hospital, arrangements were made for me to see a psychologist twice a week. Mrs. Rosen was very kind to me and tried to help me. She called my house almost every day to make sure that I was okay. I told her what went down with my stepfather, but I never told her about my uncle. I never told anybody. But things didn't get better at home. My mother was very uncomfortable about my seeing a psychologist, and my stepfather was more abusive than ever.

When I was fourteen, I decided to run away from home. One day after a real bad scene with my stepfather, I ran all the way to Brooklyn. Just as I had gotten off the Brooklyn Bridge, an older boy—about seventeen-years-old—invited me to his house. He said I could stay there as long as I wanted. I was so happy to have a place to eat and sleep that I followed him to his apartment. About a half hour after he fed me, he tried to rape me. Luckily, I managed to escape. I ran as fast as I could. When I reached the train station at the Brooklyn Bridge, I decided to kill myself. I threw myself down a flight of stairs, but only managed to hurt my head. I took the train to Bellevue Hospital, planning to get into the emergency room for my throbbing head.

But when I reached Bellevue, I decided to find something to poison myself with. I roamed around the hospital till I found an empty room with all kinds of bottles. I swallowed a whole bottle of strange pills. An hour or so later, I was still alive. I was so angry at myself. I couldn't even manage to kill myself. I just continued to roam around the hospital. Finally, I found a razor blade and slashed my wrist. The next thing I knew I woke up in a strange bed somewhere else in Bellevue. After a few days, my mother convinced me to return home with her.

I never should have. Nothing had changed. Now even my little brother was giving me a hard time. He kept on calling me "faggot" and putting me down. All his friends would make fun of me. My brother and I were in the same junior high school, and I had to fight off a bunch of twelve-year-olds just to make my way home.

Finally, I decided to run away for good. My best friend Kevin, who is gay, lived in his grandfather's empty apartment and told me I could move in with him. So instead of going home from school one day, I went to Kevin's house instead. I was nervous and scared, but glad to be out of my own house.

I lived in Kevin's apartment for three months. Kevin was real nice to me, but he wouldn't let me leave the apartment. My mother had been looking all over the Bronx for me, and Kevin didn't want her to know that I was hiding out at his place. Kevin told me that our guidance counselor kept on asking him if he knew where I was. So for three months I didn't see the light of day. I ate, slept and watched T.V. Finally, I started feeling sorry for my mom. Kevin told me that she kept on coming to school to look for me and that she'd always be crying. I decided to call her. I told her that I would see her under one condition: that she wouldn't make me return home. She agreed.

My mom and I met. She knew I was for real. She knew I was never going back home. She told me that she had contacted my birth father and that I could go and live with him and his wife. So I left Kevin's house for my father's house, but that didn't work out. I hated my father's other children. His fourteen-year-old son deals drugs, and his thirteen-year-old daughter was pregnant. I had nothing in common with them. My father's new wife hated me for taking my father away from her. Also, her house was filthy. And I didn't feel like living in a pig sty.

So after a few horrible months at my father's house, my grandfather—my father's father—was awarded guardianship of me. I've lived with him for the last year. He is wonderful and kind. He feels terrible about all that I've been through. I've tried to visit my father a few times in the past year, but no one lets me in when I knock on the door. I do speak to him on the phone all the time, and I sometimes visit him after school at the fruit stand on Pell Street where he works. I see my mother now about once a month, but I never see my stepfather. I hope I don't ever have to see him again.

Roland Jeffers
17 years old

Until I was ten years old, I lived with my grandma. My mom was too young and too messed up to take care of me. She became pregnant with me when she was fifteen years old, just a few years after she came up here from Alabama. My dad was always in and out of jail. I was the perfect kid. Seriously, my grandma used to call me her little angel. I was shy and quiet.

My problems started when I went to live with my mother. She was too busy worrying about her next high to pay any attention to me. When my father wasn't in jail, he supplied her with the dope she needed to get through the day. But when my dad was locked up, my mom used to spend her entire welfare check on drugs.

By the time I got into junior high school, I already had a bad rep. I had gotten in with the wrong crowd. I was thirteen years old, and I spent most of my time holding people up. My main turf was 163rd Street between Broadway and St. Nicholas. I used to hide a blade in my mouth. Then when I saw somebody worth rushing, I'd approach them, spit out the blade and say, "Hand it over." I was pretty good at what I did. I had a whole collection of goose jackets, gold, and sneakers.

When I was fourteen years old, I got into some pretty heavy dealing. Instead of going to school, I spent most of the day on the street corner selling crack and cocaine. I loved making money. I made between $500 to $1000 a day. My mom used to see me in the streets and threaten to put me in a home. But I knew she never would. My grandma cried a lot, and blamed my mother for what had become of me.

Then there was this big bust. It was in the news and all, and I was caught. When they were taking me away, I saw T.V. cameras. So I waved to my grandma and said, "Hello!" She told me later that she couldn't stop crying. Since I was only fifteen, I was sent to Lincoln Hall.

Lincoln Hall ain't nothing. There were no drugs or anything like you got at Spofford or Rikers. Since I wasn't doing any drugs at the time—I was just dealing them—that wasn't a problem for me. Some other niggers were going crazy. We were not even allowed to have girlfriends visiting us. Every day was the same. We slept four in a room. We'd wake up at 7 o'clock, fix our beds, brush our teeth, eat some dried-out breakfast, smoke a cigarette and go to school. After school, we spent the rest of the day fighting. Man, we fought over anything, basketballs, sneakers, even toothpaste. If some dude was lying on your bed, you'd go for him. You always had to protect your own turf. Even though we weren't supposed to have any illegal weapons, just about everybody had a razor or shank of some kind. But I gotta say that I never saw anyone get real badly cut up at Lincoln Hall.

I've been home now since September, and I've been going to George Washington High School. I plan to graduate and all. I mean if I mess up now, it's no more Lincoln Hall. Since I'm seventeen, I'd go straight to Rikers. And I don't really wanna deal with that scene.

Diane Smith
16 years old

I grew up in a large apartment in Canarsie. We even had a back-yard. But then we had to leave. My two older brothers were dealing cocaine. They ended up owing the wrong people money, and our lives were being threatened. One evening, four men knocked on our door, demanded money and threatened to kill us if we didn't come up with it. My mother and I left.

My brothers had always been in trouble. They are only nine months apart and do everything together. They were picked up for robbery when they were ten and sent to a juvenile deten-tion center upstate. They spent most of their early teen years in Spofford and they have been in and out of Rikers ever since.

My brothers were soon sent back to Rikers, and my mother and I lost our apartment. For two years we went from one friend's house to another. It was terrible. All my mother's so-called friends took advantage of her. They took her money and stole what little we had. Whenever my mom brought food into their house for her and me, it disappeared.

Finally we were given a room at Bayview Marina, a welfare hotel in Sheepshead Bay. It really wasn't bad. It was a lot better than living with my mother's friends and getting ripped off by them. Also, it was clean. For the first time, I felt safe. But after we'd been there a few months, the Bureau of Child Welfare decided that I should go live with my father. My mother then had to leave Bayview, since it was only for families.

I was thirteen when I went to live with my father. It was horrible. I'd only seen my father once before when I was eleven. My father would get drunk almost every night and rape me. I hated it, but I didn't know what to do. My father kept on saying, "You're mine. I can do what I want with you." I had no where to go. This went on for about a year. Finally, I told my mother what was going on. Even though she blamed me, she got me out of my father's house.

My mother and I were then put into a shelter on Catherine Street. I was glad to be away from my father, but I hated the shelter. My father had made me feel so dirty, and here I couldn't even take a shower without being eaten by crabs and lice. There were drug addicts everywhere, and people would attack each other for a cigarette.

Two months ago we were moved to a hotel in Queens. Even though there are no crack addicts around, it's pretty awful here. There are rats everywhere and people always ready to fight about nothing. We have no phone and we can't have any visitors.

I haven't made any friends since we left our apartment in Canarsie. I'm just too embarrassed by the way we've been living. I feel that people are always staring at me. I feel that they can look right through me and know everything about me. My mother's constantly on my back about going to school. But when I come to school, I can't concentrate. I used to like it, but that was when I was in junior high school.

My two brothers are due to be out on probation soon, but my mom has given up on them. They've never kicked their cocaine habits. Their girlfriends smuggle the stuff to them all the time. The coke is either hidden in their babies' pampers or snuck over in a kiss. The security is weak, and the guards turn the other way.

My mom dumps on me a lot. She doesn't really understand how hard the last few years have been on me. She is now suing my father. It's not because she feels so bad about what he did to me. It's just that now she finally has a way of getting back at him for dumping on her.

I feel that all I've been through has made me kind of crazy. Just last Friday I started seeing a counselor from an organization called "Women Against Rape." The counselor had also been raped by her father. She understood me, and I felt a lot better after getting it off my chest.

But what I'd really like to do now is join Mickey Mouse in Disneyland.

A Glossary of Current
Street Slang

B

base—v. to smoke cocaine: I was *basin'* today.

bite—v. to copy someone else's style: Don't *bite*!

bliss—n. any smoke that gets you high: Let's go buy some *bliss*.

blisted—adj. high: I was *blisted* for hours.

blow—n. cocaine: Let's sniff some *blow*!

blow up—v. to leave: *Blow up*! The cops are coming.

blunt—n. cigar with marijuana: I smoked a *blunt*.

bomb—v. to write on trains: I used to *bomb* all the trains.

booty—adj. weak: That nigger's *booty*.

bottles—n. crack-filled vials: Got any *bottles*?

break night—v. to stay up all night. I was *breakin' night*.

break out—v. to leave: I'm *breakin' out*.

buckin' off—v. shooting guns: The drug dealers were *buckin' off* last night.

buddah—n. a mild type of marijuana: Got any *buddah*, man?

buff—v. to erase: He *buffed* my tag.

buggin'—v. acting crazy: She sure is *buggin'*.

bum rushin'—v. acting wild: The nigger was *bum rushin'*.

bust a cap—v. to shoot someone: Did ya *bust a cap*?

C

caesar—n. closely shaved haircut with lines: Check out his *caesar*.

cess—n. weed: That *cess* got me buggin'.

chill—v. to relax: adj. great, stylish: I need to *chill*. Those jeans are *chill*.

chocolate thai—n. high quality marijuana: The *chocolate thai* got me nice.

C.O.C.—excl. cops on corner: *C.O.C.*! Let's split.

cold chillin—v. relaxing to the maximum: I was *cold chillin'* last night.

cooly—n. cigarette mixed with cocaine: Let's go puff a *cooly*.

crew—n. group: I was chillin' with the *crew*.

crib—n. house: I'll meet ya at my *crib*.

crisp—n. crack with weed: You got that *crisp*?

D

dap—adj. stylish: You lookin' *dap*, bro.

def—adj. great: The jam was *def*!

deuce—n. two-dollar bottle of crack: Got the *deuce*, bro?

diesel—adj. strong, muscular: Joe is *diesel*.

dime—n. ten-dollar bottle of crack: Got any *dimes*?

dip—v. to leave: I gotta *dip*.

dis—v. to put down; to disrespect: Don't *dis* me, man.

dividends—n. money: All she wants is the *dividends*.

dope—adj. great, stylish: That shirt is *dope*.

down—adj. ready for action: Yo, man, I'm *down*!

d.t.—n. undercover cop: He was busted by the *d.t.*

dusted—adj. high: I got *dusted* last night.

F

feanin'—v. to want something real badly, to crave: The nigger's *feanin'* for some crack.

five-o—n. cops: I saw the *five-o* coming up my block.

flip—v. to fight: Me and my homeboy were *flippin'*.

foolish—adj. great: You lookin' *foolish* tonight.

freakin'—v. to dance real close: He was *freakin'* me last night.

freebase—v. to smoke cocaine: Wanna *freebase*?

fresh—adj. see *dope*: That jacket is *fresh*.

front—v. to back down: Why you *frontin'*, man?

G

gear—n. clothes: She wears fly *gear*.

get busy—v. to fight; to make love: Let's *get busy*!

get fat—v. to make money; He be *gettin' fat*.

get knocked—v. to get arrested: Don't *get knocked*.

get paid in full—v. to rob someone: It's time to *get paid in full*.

H

hawk—v. to check out with the intent to steal: Stop *hawking* my gold.

heat—v. to tease someone: Why you *heatin'* on me?

hoe—n. slut: Don't mess with that *hoe*.

homeboy—n. close friend: J.T. is my *homeboy*.

homegirl—n. see *homeboy*: She's always with her *homegirl*.

hype—the greatest, better than *dope*: Yo, that sweater is *hype*.

I

ice—v. to punch someone in the face: He tried to *ice* me.

illin'—v. acting crazy: You be *illin'*.

Indica—n. powerful marijuana: I bought a bag of *Indica*.

iron—n. gun: What kinda *iron* you got?

J

jammies—n. sneakers, any outfit: I bought some fly *jammies*.

jam—n. party with loud music: I met her at the *jam*.

jocking—v. following: Why you *jocking* me, man?

joint—n. gun: Down in Phillie, the *joints* are cheap.

jumbs—n. crack-filled vials: Gotta get me some *jumbs*.

K

kick the ballistics—v. to engage in conversation; to rap: We *kicked the ballistics* all night.

kicks—n. sneakers: Those *kicks* are fresh!

knock the boots—v. to have sex: I've been *knockin' the boots*.

L

lamping—v. see *chilling*: I'm just *lamping*.

lay-up—n. the place where the trains are kept: We bombed the trains at the Bowery *lay-up*.

M

mamaduke—n. mom: I'm not messing with *mamaduke*.

max—v. to relax: My homeboy was *maxin'*.

money dog—n. see *homeboy*: Yo, *money dog*, let's break out!

moist—adj. weak: Your homeboy's *moist*.

N

nicks—n. five-dollar bottles of crack: He be dealing *nicks*.

nigger—n. any guy: The *nigger* was zooted.

O

on a mission—acting crazy: You must be *on a mission*.

on the strength—I agree: *On the strength*, man.

P

perico—n. cocaine: He's zooted on *perico*.

piece—n. a pistol: I have my *piece* on me.

posse—n. a group of people, a gang of youths: The *posse* plans to jump him.

punk—n. a weak person: He's a *punk*.

R

riff—v. to start trouble: Why you *riffin'* with me, man?

rocks—n. cut-up cocaine: Let's sniff some *rocks*.

roll—v. to beat up: I *rolled* your homeboy.

rush—n. the effect of a drug: v. to fight; to attack: I caught a *rush* after I sniffed coke. Let's *rush* him.

S

scheme—v. to watch someone closely: Don't be *scheming* on me.

scramblin'—v. to sell drugs: He's *scramblin'* on the corner.

shooby—n. cocaine: Got some *shooby*?

shoot joints—v. to fight: I was *shootin' joints* last night.

skeezer—a person who has sex with everybody: She's a real *skeezer*.

ski—n. cocaine: Let's get some *ski*.

skied up—adj. high on cocaine: I was *skied up* all night.

skunk—n. a strong type of marijuana: Let's light up some *skunk*.

slammin'—adj. great: That song is *slammin'*.

snuff—v. to sneak up on someone for the purpose of attacking him: I'm gonna *snuff* that punk.

soft—adj. weak: That punk is *soft*.

splif—n. long joint: I rolled a *splif*.

squallie—n. girl: The *squallies* look fly.

strapped—adj. laden with guns: He was *strapped* last night.

step off—v. to walk away, leave: I told her to *step off*.

stomp—v. to beat up: I should have *stomped* him.

stupid fresh—adj. excellent: His piece is *stupid fresh*!

sweatin'—v. admiring: He be *sweatin'* me.

sucker—n. a person too scared to fight: I'm gonna rush that *sucker*.

system—n. jail: I was up at the *system* last night.

T

tag—v. to write one's name graffiti-style; n. one's name: J.T. *tagged* the newly painted walls. His *tag* is everywhere.

tax—v. to steal: I'm gonna *tax* that box.

time out—stop selling; the cops are coming: *Time out*, bro!

toast—n. a gun: Do you know where I can get a *toast*?

toolie—n. a gun: He went to get his *toolie*.

toy—n. a weak graffiti writer: J.T. is a *toy*.

tres—n. three-dollar bottle of crack: Got any *tres*?

Tyrone—n. a powerful strain of marijuana: Yo, let's pick up *Tyrone*.

W

wack—adj. of poor quality: His piece was *wack*.

wax—v. to hurt: I didn't mean to *wax* him.

weak—adj. opposite of *fresh*: That jacket is *weak*.

wife—n. girlfriend: Don't mess with my *wife*.

wildin'—v. acting crazy: Stop *wildin'*.

woola—n. crack and herb rolled into a joint: Got any *woola*?

word—excl. I agree: *Word*! His tag is weak.

writing partner—n. person with whom you do graffiti: I went bombing with my *writing partner*.

Z

zooted—adj. high: I got *zooted* last night.

Where to Get Help

AIDS

The following telephone hotlines offer information and referral services:

Public Health Service National AIDS Hotline
1-800-342-AIDS
1-800-342-2437

National Gay Task Force AIDS Information Hotline
1-800-221-7044

Hetrick-Martin Institute, Inc.
Serving Gay and Lesbian Youth
401 West Street
New York, NY 10014
(212) 633-8920

For AIDS information and referrals:

National AIDS/ARC Epidemiological Network
2676 N. Halsted Street
Chicago, IL 60614
(312) 943-6600

National AIDS Research and Education Foundation
54 10th Street
San Francisco, CA 94013
(415) 626-8784

AIDS Action Council
Federation of AIDS-Related Organizations
729 8th Street, SE, Suite 200
Washington DC 2003
(202) 547-3101

Lambda Legal Defense and Education Fund
666 Broadway
New York, NY 10012
(212) 995-8585

Alcoholism

For information and referrals:

Children of Alcoholics Foundation, Inc.
540 Madison Avenue
New York, NY 10022
(212) 980-5860

National Institute on Alcohol Abuse and Alcoholism (NIAAA)
Room 11-05
Parklawn Building
5600 Fishers Lane
Rockville, MD 20852

Alcoholics Anonymous World Services
P.O. Box 459
Grand Central Station
New York, NY 10163
(212) 686-1100

Al-Anon Family Group Headquarters
P.O. Box 182
Madison Square Station
New York, NY 10010
(212) 481-6565

Alcohol Education for Youth
1500 Western Avenue
Albany, NY 12203

Alcoholism and Drug Dependency Council, Inc
1 Kings Highway North
Westport, CT 06880

Mothers Against Drunk Driving
5330 Primrose, Suite 146
Fair Oaks, CA 95628

National Clearing House for Alcohol Information
P.O. Box 2345
Rockville, MD 20852

Alcohol and Drug Problems Association of North America
1101 15th Street, NW
Suite 204
Washington, DC 20005

National Center for Alcohol Education
1601 N. Kent Street
Arlington, VA 22209

Drug Abuse

The following telephone hotlines offer information and referral services:

National Institute on Drug Abuse hotline:
1-800-662-HELP

Cocaine Hotline
1-800-COCAINE

Hale House Center
1-800-235-4433

For literature on drug abuse:

National Clearinghouse for Alcohol and Drug Information
P.O. Box 2345
Rockville, MD 20852
(301) 468-2600

National Council for Drug Education
204 Monroe Street
Rockville, MD 20850
(301) 294-0600

National Federation of Parents for Drug-Free Youth
8730 Georgia Avenue, Suite 200
Silver Spring, MD 20910
1-800-554-KIDS

Cocaine Center
152 Lombard
San Francisco, CA
1-415-392-1658

National Self-Help Clearinghouse
33 W. 42nd Street
New York, NY 10036

Homelessness

For information on programs for the homeless:

National Coalition for the Homeless
1439 Rhode Island Avenue, NW
Washington, DC 20005
(202) 659-3319
&
105 E. 22nd Street
New York, NY 10010
(212) 460-8110

National Union for the Homeless
2001 Spring Garden Street
Philadelphia, PA 19130

Homeless Information Exchange
1830 Connecticut Avenue, NW
Washington, DC 20009
(202) 462-7551

Pregnancy

The following telephone hotline offers referrals to abortion clinics:

National Abortion Federation
1-800-223-0618

For referrals for treatment, counseling and abortion services:

National Women's Health Organization
1-800-221-2568

For leads to private non-profit agencies that run group maternity homes and maternity care centers:

Family Service Association of America
44 E. 23rd Street
New York, NY 10010
(212) 674-6100

Runaways

The following telephone hotlines offer information on referral services:

National Runaway Switchboard
Metro—Help, Inc.,
2210 N. Halsted Street
Chicago, IL 60614
1-800-621-4000

Runaway Hotline
P.O. Box 52896
Houston, Texas 77052
1-800-231-6946

Covenant House
460 W. 41st Street
New York, NY 10036
1-800-999-9999

National Center for Missing/Exploited Children
1-800-843-5678

Sexual Abuse

The following hotline offers referrals to services and resources in every state 24 hours a day, 7 days a week:

Childhelp USA
6463 Independence Avenue
Woodland Hills, CA 91367
1-800-4-A-CHILD
1-800-422-4453

For referrals to local self-help groups for parents and children:

Parents Anonymous
7120 Franklin Avenue
Los Angeles, CA 90046
1-800-421-0353

For referrals to Rape Crisis Centers and hotlines:

Pennsylvania Coalition Against Rape
2200 N. 3rd Street
Harrisburg, PA 17110
(717) 232-6745

Anti-Social and Violent Behavior Center
(301) 443-3728

National Organization for Victim Assistance (NOVA)
(718) 232-8560

Suicide

For referrals and information:

Youth Suicide National Center
1825 Eye Street, NW, Suite 400
Washington, DC 20006
(202) 429-2016

Parents Involved Network (PIN)
Mental Health Assn. of Southeastern Pennsylvania
311 S. Juniper Street
Philadelphia, PA 19107

American Society for Adolescent Psychiatry
24 Green Valley Road
Wallingford, PA 19086
(215) 566-1054

National Save-A-Life League
815 2nd Avenue, Suite 409
New York, NY 10017
(212) 736-6191

Annotated Bibliography

AIDS

Hyde, Margaret O. and Forsyth, Elizabeth H. *AIDS: What Does It Mean to You*. New York: Walker & Company, 1987.

AIDS is defined and explained in language that is accessible to the adolescent. Teenagers are taught how to avoid AIDS. Epidemic diseases of the past are discussed. The dangers of ungrounded fear regarding AIDS transmission are considered. The lack of danger of transmission of AIDS from casual contact is stressed. Compassion is urged towards the AIDS victim.

Levert, Suzanne. *AIDS: In Search of a Killer*. New York: Simon and Shuster, 1987.

Theories on the origin of AIDS are presented. The high-risk groups are identified. The effect of AIDS on the body is discussed. The search for a cure is documented. The precautions we can take to protect ourselves from the disease are presented. The case studies included offer perspective on the AIDS' patients feelings of fear and guilt. A useful glossary defining all AIDS related terms is included.

Nourse, Alan E. *AIDS*. New York: Franklin Watts, 1986.

The possible origins, symptoms and characteristics of AIDS are discussed. The ongoing search for a cure is documented. Questions to dispel myths and fears concerning the epidemic are answered. Maps and graphs document the incidence of AIDS by age group, race, ethnic group and sexual orientation.

Silverstein, Alvin and Virginia. *AIDS: Deadly Threat*. Hillside, New Jersey: Enslow Publishers, 1986.

The facts of AIDS are discussed so that the spread of the disease can be prevented among young people. Young people are advised what to do should their blood be tested positive for AIDS antibodies. The impact of AIDS worldwide is considered. The controversy over whether children with AIDS should be allowed to attend school is discussed.

Wachter, Oralee. *Sex, Drugs, and AIDS*. New York: Bantam, 1987.

Based on the award-winning documentary, this candid guide is directed at young people. The focus is on the transmission of the AIDS virus and the importance of safe sex. Young people are also made aware of the danger of sharing needles. Assurance is given to the young reader that the AIDS infection can be easily avoided.

Whitmore, George. *Someone Was Here: Profiles in the AIDS Epidemic*. New York: New American Library, 1988.

Three years in the AIDS epidemic are covered from the perspective of a journalist, himself an AIDS victim. Insights are given into the feelings and thoughts of people infected with the AIDS virus. The devastating effect AIDS has on families is documented in the final section of this book entitled "Lincoln Hospital, South Bronx."

Alcoholism and Drug Abuse

Bartimole, Carmella R. and Bartimole, John E. *Teenage Alcoholism & Substance Abuse: Causes, Consequences and Cures*. Hollywood, Florida: Frederick Fell, 1987.

The reasons that teens become involved with drugs and alcohol are explored. Parents are offered techniques to diminish their teen's vulnerability to substance abuse. Tell-tale signs of substance abuse are identified. Detailed steps in getting help are presented. Schools are urged to adopt effective drug education programs.

Ketcham, Katherine and Gustafson, Ginny Lyford. *Living on the Edge: A Guide to Intervention for Families with Drug and Alcohol Problems*. New York: Bantam, 1989.

Practical methods of intervention for families who seek recovery from the effects of alcohol and drug abuse are presented. A directory on adolescent drug use and an appendix of drug facts are included. Case studies are presented, along with a questionnaire to determine the dependent's stage of addiction.

Newman, Susan. *You Can Say No to a Drink or a Drug*. New York: Putnam, 1986.

Preteens and teenagers are taught how to resist alcohol and drugs. They are shown how to get out of difficult alcohol or drug situations. Ten photographs illustrate scenarios with which teens will identify. The readers are taught what they can expect in terms of peer pressure and how to resist it. Also presented are the hard facts about drugs and alcohol from hangovers to auto accidents.

Ward, Brian R. *Alcohol Abuse*. New York: Franklin Watts, 1987.

Young people are introduced to the dangers of alcohol. The short and long-term effects of alcohol are discussed. The appeal of alcohol to the young is analyzed. Young readers are taught how to recognize and treat a drinking problem. A glossary of terms related to alcohol abuse is included. Colorful illustrations supplement the text.

Woods, Geraldine and Harold. *Cocaine*. New York: Franklin Watts, 1985.

Young people are introduced to cocaine and its effects. The dangers of cocaine use are presented. The history of this potent drug is explored. The variety of treatments for cocaine abuse is discussed. A glossary defining words related to the use and trade of cocaine is included.

Domestic Abuse

Fontana, Vincent J. *Somewhere a Child Is Crying: Maltreatment—Causes and Prevention*. New York: New American Library, 1983.

Child abuse is presented as a serious societal and medical problem. The failure of society to come to grips with the devastating effects of child abuse is documented. New laws and new approaches in treating both the abusive parents and the battered child are prescribed.

Gelles, Richard J. and Strauss, Murray A. *Intimate Violence: The Definitive Study of the Causes and Consequences of Abuse in the American Family.* New York: Simon and Schuster, 1988.

The focus is on family violence. Case studies of child battering, wife beating, abuse of the elderly, and violence between siblings are presented. Insights into the types of relationships that permit violence are given. The consequences of living in a violent home are examined. Changes that must take place and programs that must be implemented are suggested.

Homelessness

Gorder, Cheryl. *Homeless! Without Addresses in America.* Temple, Arizona: Blue Bird Publishing, 1988.

Homelessness is presented as the social crisis of the decade. Common myths about the homeless are dispelled. The reasons behind homelessness are explained. Possible solutions are proposed. The plight of homeless runaways is vividly depicted. Each of us is urged to help in our own way. Pictures and graphs supplement the text.

Kaufman, Curt and Gita. *Hotel Boy.* New York: Atheneum, 1987.

The plight of two homeless brothers and their mom is presented from the point of view of a young child. A family who lost everything in a fire is living in a crowded room in a welfare hotel. The difficulties faced by the mom and her two sons are vividly and sympathetically depicted in this story for school-age children.

Kozol, Jonathan. *Rachel and Her Children: Homeless Families in America.* New York: Ballantine, 1989.

The lives of a dozen families and their children are depicted. Based on conversations with residents of welfare hotels and shelters in New York City, this book is the most definitive study of the homeless to date.

Landau, Elaine. *The Homeless.* New York: Simon and Schuster, 1987.

The origins of the new homelessness are explored. The diverse groups of individuals who make up the new homeless are discussed. Case histories of homeless people are included. The sordid conditions of public shelters are vividly portrayed. The special problems of homeless youth are addressed.

Pregnancy

Barr, Linda and Monserrat, Catherine. *Teenage Pregnancy: A New Beginning.* Albuquerque, New Mexico: New Futures, 1983.

Pregnant teenagers are taught what to expect in the course of pregnancy and childbirth. Reactions of teens to finding out they are pregnant are included. The workings of the female and male reproductive systems are explained in simple terms. Sexually transmitted diseases are discussed and advice is given on how to avoid them. Teenagers are presented with questions to ask themselves before getting married.

————. *Working with Childbearing Adolescents.* Albuquerque, New Mexico: New Futures, 1986.

General strategy and methodology in dealing with the pregnant teenager are presented. The conflicts and unique challenges faced by teenage parents are considered. The qualities that will enhance the effectiveness of counselors who work with pregnant teens are discussed. Lesson plans are included.

Bode, Janet. *Kids Having Kids: The Unwed Teenage Parent.* New York: Franklin Watts, 1980.

The actual experiences of young women and their attitudes towards sexuality, birth control and pregnancy are examined. Adoption as a viable option is discussed. Teenage readers are presented with the problems that young parents must face when raising a child alone.

Dash, Leon. *When Children Want Children: The Urban Crisis of Teen-age Childbearing.* New York: Morrow, 1989.

The thoughts and experiences of poor, black teenagers in Washington Highlands, one of Washington D.C.'s poorest neighborhoods, are documented here. Their motivations for becoming parents are examined. The nature of black family life in the rural South is explored.

Ewy, Donna and Rodger. *Teen Pregnancy: The Challenges We Faced, the Choices We Made.* Boulder, Colorado: Pruett Publishing Company, 1984.

First person narratives on what it means to be a teenage parent are presented to teens facing pregnancy. Teen parents discuss the special problems they faced. Information on nutrition, childbirth, infant care and birth control is presented. The importance of finishing school is stressed.

Richards, Arlene Kramer and Willis, Irene. *What to Do If You or Someone You Know Is Under 18 and Pregnant.* New York: Lothrop, Lee, and Shephard Books, 1983.

Information for the pregnant teen on sex, birth control, pregnancy and childbirth is presented. Abortion is discussed as a natural option. The difficulties of an early marriage are realistically portrayed. Included in the final section is a useful list of adolescent clinics, maternity and adoption services in every state.

Runaways

Landau, Elaine. *On the Streets: The Lives of Adolescent Prostitutes.* New York: Simon and Schuster, 1987.

Based on the author's interviews, profiles of young prostitutes are featured. The sordid details of their daily lives are presented. The role of the pimp is considered. The historical background of prostitution is discussed.

Madison, Arnold. *Runaway Teens: An American Tragedy.* New York: Elsevier/Nelson, 1979.

Written primarily for young people, the frank portrayal of the plight of runaways should discourage potential runaways. A useful chapter which profiles the potential runaway should be of special interest to parents and counselors. Various reasons for running away are discussed. Case studies from a variety of social and economic backgrounds are presented.

Sexual Abuse

Adams, Caren, Fay, Jennifer and Loreen-Martin, Jan. *No Is Not Enough: Helping Teenagers Avoid Sexual Assault*. San Luis Obispo, California: Impact Books, 1984.

Parents are taught how to protect their children from sexual assault and exploitation. Some of the misconceptions teens have about sex are discussed. Parents are offered concrete hints on how to build their teen's self-esteem. Options open to parents should their child become a victim of sexual abuse are discussed. The influence of media in determining our sexual attitudes is analyzed.

Cooney, Judith. *Coping With Sexual Abuse*. New York: Rosen Publishing Group, 1987.

The myths and effects of sexual abuse are the focus here. Young adults are informed of the resources available to them. Victims of abuse are urged to seek help. Discussion topics follow each chapter make this a valuable guide to teachers and counselors.

Crewdson, John. *By Silence Betrayed: Sexual Abuse of Children in America*. Boston: Little Brown and Company, 1988.

The impact of sexual abuse on its young victims is studied. The causes of sexual abuse are analyzed. The most effective ways to prosecute perpetrators are presented. The effectiveness of therapy upon the perpetrators is considered. The disturbing recent problem of paid child workers who sexually abuse children is discussed.

Forward, Susan and Buck, Craig. *Betrayal of Innocence: Incest and Its Devastation*. New York: Penguin, 1978.

Incest is explored from the perspective of a social worker, herself an incest victim. Twenty-five case histories explore the traumatic effects of incest. Its causes and consequences are analyzed. This easy-to-read book is valuable to laymen, as well as to professionals.

Goodwin, Jean. *Sexual Abuse: Incest Victims and Their Families*. Boston: John Wright, 1982.

The recognition, prevention, and treatment of incest are discussed. Insights into the pathology of dysfunctional families are provided. Direct quotations from family members and drawings done by victimized children are analyzed.

Counselors are provided with guidelines in talking with families of incest victims.

Haden, Dawn C. *Out of Harm's Way: Readings on Child Sexual Abuse, Its Prevention and Treatment.* Phoenix, Arizona: Oryx Press, 1986.

Articles reprinted from various publications on the theme of child abuse make up this book. Strategies for the prevention of child abuse are presented. Identification and treatment of the sexually abused youngster are discussed. The annotated bibliography of books and audiovisual materials is of special value to teachers and counselors.

Herman, Judith Lewis. *Father–Daughter Incest.* Cambridge: Harvard University Press, 1981.

The focus is on father–daughter relationships. The destructiveness of incest upon its powerless victims is vividly portrayed. Valuable insights are provided into the minds of incestuous fathers and dysfunctional mothers. A lengthy appendix with incest statues of every state is included.

Kempe, Ruth S. and C. Henry. *The Common Secret: Sexual Abuse of Children and Adolescents.* New York: W.H. Freeman and Company, 1984.

The impact of sexual abuse upon all those who have to deal with it is discussed. The causes for its recent increase are analyzed. The different categories of sexual abuse are defined. Case studies dispute many of the myths surrounding sexual abuse. An appendix listing educational materials and additional books on the subject is particularly useful.

Kosof, Anna. *Incest: Families in Crisis.* New York: Franklin Watts, 1985.

The impact of incest on the victim is discussed. The characteristics of an incestuous family are presented. Interviews with victims and family members provide insights into the prevention and treatment of incest. Information on sources for help throughout the United States and Canada is given in a lengthy appendix.

Parrot, Andrea. *Coping With Date Rape & Acquaintance Rape.* New York: Rosen Publishing Group, 1988.

Young people are urged to confront the reality of acquaintance rape. Myths about rape are dispelled. The factors that lead to date or acquaintance rape are considered. Advice on how to cope with the aftermath of acquaintance rape is given. A useful appendix of glossary of terms related to rape is included.

Terkel, Susan N. and Rench, Janice E. *Feeling Safe, Feeling Strong: How to Avoid Sexual Abuse and What to Do If It Happens to You.* Minneapolis: Lerner Publications Company, 1984.

Six personal narratives depict the variety of forms sexual abuse of the young can take. Pornography, exhibitionism, incest and rape are defined in simple language that is accessible to young readers. Victims are urged to talk about their experiences to an adult whom they can trust.

Suicide

Chiles, John. *Teenage Suicide and Depression.* New York: Chelsea House, 1986.

The focus is on the roles drugs play in the emotional upheavals that teenagers experience. The effect drugs have on mood is explored. Youngsters learn what happens once a drug enters their body. The pressures that result in serious depression and suicide are discussed. Advice is offered to the potentially suicidal teen.

Greenberg, Harvey R. *Hanging In: What You Should Know About Psychotherapy.* New York: Four Winds Press, 1982

Common emotional problems of adolescence are discussed. The processes of adolescent physical and psychological growth are described. The typical situations and symptoms that bring adolescents into psychotherapy are presented. Practical advice on getting the kind of professional help that is needed is given. Adolescents are familiarized with the different types of psychotherapy available to them.

Hafen, Brent Q. and Frandsen, Kathryn J. *Youth Suicide: Depression and Loneliness.* Evergreen, Colorado: Cordillera Press, 1989.

Factors that contribute to teenage suicide are discussed. Myths regarding suicide are dispelled. Warning signs and symptoms are presented. Parents and teachers are given sound advice in recognizing and dealing with the suicidal youngster.

Hermes, Patricia. *A Time to Listen: Preventing Youth Suicide.* New York: Harcourt Brace Jovanovich, 1987.

Guidelines for when and how to intervene with suicidal youngsters are presented. The roles of drugs, parental pressure, rock music lyrics, and suicide publicity are discussed. The importance of communication in preventing teen suicide is stressed. The special problems faced by friends left behind are considered.

Leder, Jane Mersky. *Dead Serious: A Book for Teenagers About Teenage Suicide.* New York: Atheneum, 1987.

The effect of teenage suicide on family and friends is discussed. Early reactions, as well as later feelings, are considered. Possible reasons for the increase in teen suicide are presented. Friends of suicidal teens are given concrete advice. Case histories and interviews with teens who have attempted suicide are included.

Rosenberg, Terry. "Handling a Suicide Crisis," *Children and Adolescents with Mental Illness: A Parent's Guide*, ed. Evelyn McElroy. Kensington: Woodbine House, 1987.

Twenty factors that would label a teenager a high suicide risk are identified. Parents are taught how to recognize depression in their youngster. They are given valuable insights into what may motivate their youngster to contemplate suicide. The role of family stress is emphasized. The importance of communicating with the suicidal child, as well as securing the proper professional help, is stressed.